CW00427927

A GUIDE TO
THE EMPLOYMENT ACTS

LAW AT WORK

Other Books in the Series

HANDLING REDUNDANCY
Sue Morris

INDUSTRIAL TRIBUNALS
Philip Parry

MANAGING THE PENSIONS REVOLUTION
Sue Ward

THE NEW EMPLOYMENT CONTRACT
Patricia Leighton and Aidan ODonnell

UNFAIR DISMISSAL
Richard Painter

THE WORK ENVIRONMENT
Patricia Leighton

A GUIDE TO
THE EMPLOYMENT ACTS
NEW EDITION

JOAN HENDERSON

Introduction by Professor
Patricia Leighton

NICHOLAS BREALEY
PUBLISHING

LONDON

This revised edition first published by
Nicholas Brealey Publishing Limited in 1995
21 Bloomsbury Way
London WC1A 2TH

New edition 1990, revised 1992, new edition 1994

ISBN 1 85788 038 2

© Joan Henderson 1990, 1991, 1992, 1994, 1995

British Library Cataloguing-in-publication Data
A catalogue record for this book is available from the
British Library.

All rights reserved. No part of this publication may be
reproduced, stored in a retrieval system or transmitted,
in any form or by any means, electronic, mechanical,
photocopying, recording and/or otherwise without the
prior written permission of the publishers. This may not
be lent, resold, hired out or otherwise disposed of by the
way of trade in any form, binding or cover other than
that in which it is published, without prior consent of
the publishers.

*The Publisher accepts no responsibility for errors of
commission or omission.*

Typeset by August Filmsetting, Haydock, St Helens
Printed and bound in Great Britain by Redwood Books

CONTENTS

PREFACE   9

The Trade Union Reform and Employment Rights   11
    Act 1993

INTRODUCTION   13

PART I Individual Rights   21

The Employment Protection (Consolidation) Act 1978
The Transfer of Undertakings (Protection of
    Employment) Regulations 1981
The Employment Acts 1980, 1989 and 1990
The Trade Union and Labour Relations
    (Consolidation) Act 1992
The Trade Union Reform and Employment Rights
    Act 1993

Written information to be supplied by   22
    employers
        Written particulars of terms of employment   22
        Itemised pay statement   24
        Written statement of reasons for dismissal   26
        Written explanation of redundancy pay   28

Wage payment   30
        Methods of payment   30
        Deductions from wages   30
        Guarantee payments   32
        Employer's insolvency   36
        Wages councils   36

Maternity rights   38
  General right to maternity leave   38
  Right of those with two years' service   40
  Time off for antenatal care   42
  Dismissal on grounds of pregnancy   44
  Suspension on maternity grounds   44

Time off rights   46
  Trade union duties and activities   46
  Public duties   46
  Looking for work   48
  Suspension on medical grounds   48
  Maternity   50
  Infringement of time off right   50

Periods of notice   52

Unfair dismissal   54
  Fairness   54
  Unfairness   56
  Complaints to industrial tribunals   58
  Reinstatement and re-engagement   60
  Compensation   62
  Exemption for approved procedures   64

Redundancy payments   68
  Offers of further employment   70
  Employees leaving before their notice expires   70
  Strikes during notice   72
  Lay-offs and short time   72
  Making a claim   74
  Rebates to employers   74
  Exemption for approved schemes   74

Transfer of undertakings   76

Continuity of employment   80
  Application of rules   80
  Part-timers rights   82
  Temporary employees   82

PART II Collective rights 83

The Transfer of Undertakings (Protection of
  Employment) Regulations 1981
The Trade Union and Labour Relations
  (Consolidation) Act 1992
The Trade Union Reform and Employment Rights
  Act 1993

Trade unions 84
  Definitions 84
  Ballots and elections 86
  Election of union executive committees 88
  Trade union affairs 90

Trade union membership 92
  The right to membership 92
  Obligations of employers 92
  Obligations of unions 96
  Union membership requirements in contracts 98

Collective bargaining 100
  Recognition of trade unions 100
  Collective agreements 100
  Codes of Practice 104

Disclosure of information 106
  General duty 106
  Information on redundancies 108
  Information on transfer of business 108

Procedures for handling redundancies 112
  Consultation 112
  Notification 114
  Failure to comply 114
  Collective agreements on redundancies 116

Industrial action   118
   Trade dispute   118
   Immunities   120
   Ballots before industrial action   122
   Picketing   124
   Union liability   126
   Remedies   126

PART III Machinery   131

**The Trade Union and Labour Relations
(Consolidation) Act 1992
The Trade Union Reform and Employment Rights
Act 1993**

The Advisory, Conciliation and Arbitration Service   132
Industrial tribunals   134
The Employment Appeal Tribunal   136
The Central Arbitration Committee   136
The Certification Officer   138
The Commissioner for Rights of Trade Union Members   138
The Commissioner for Protection Against Unlawful   140
   Industrial Action

Index   141

PREFACE

This revised edition includes the changes to part timers' rights, which are now, broadly, the same as full timers and notes the Sunday Trading Act, 1994. The book is in two main parts – one dealing with individual rights, derived principally from the Employment Protection (Consolidation) Act 1978, as later amended, and one dealing with collective rights, arising mainly from the Trade Union and Labour Relations (Consolidation) Act 1992 as amended. This distinction is not a clear-cut one since some of the law affecting collective rights and collective bargaining springs from the individual right to belong (or not to belong) to an independent trade union, and the individual right not to be penalised for trade union activities. For this reason the book contains many cross-references.

The following abbreviations are used (those in brackets are used in margins):

ACAS	The Advisory, Conciliation and Arbitration Service
EA80 (E)	Employment Act 1980
EA89 (4E)	Employment Act 1989
EA90 (5E)	Employment Act 1990
EAT	Employment Appeal Tribunal
EP(C)A(EPC)	Employment Protection (Consolidation) Act 1978
PTER (PT)	Part-time Employees (Employment Protection) Regulations 1995
STA (ST)	Sunday Trading Act 1994

TLR(C) (T)   Trade Union and Labour Relations (Consoli-
                dation) Act 1992

TUER (TE)   Trade Union Reform and Employment
                Rights Act 1993

TUPE   Transfer of Undertakings (Protection of
                Employment) Regulations 1981

WA   Wages Act 1986

Trade Union Reform and Employment Rights Act 1993

Much of the 1993 Act was necessary in order to implement EC Directives and to respond to case law. Below is a summary of the main changes introduced by the Act.

Employee rights

TE 29 1 It is automatically unfair to dismiss an employee for exercising statutory employment rights, regardless of length of service or hours of work.

TE 26 2 Additional details have to be included in the employee's written statement of terms and conditions of employment.

TE 23 3 Women are entitled to 14 weeks' maternity leave regardless of their length of service or hours of work.

TE 28 4 Employees are protected from being penalised for carrying out legitimate health and safety activities, regardless of length of service or hours of work.

TE 33 5 The Regulations governing business transfers (TUPE) are extended to cover non-commercial undertakings.

Trade unions

TE 14 6 Individuals are given the right to join the union of their choice, and employers the right to offer inducements to employees to opt out of collective bargaining.

TE 15 7 The automatic deduction of union dues from pay must be authorised in writing by the employees every three years.

TE 34 8 The duty of an employer to inform and consult union representatives about collective redundancies is made more specific.

Industrial action

TE 17
9 Strike ballots must be postal and independently scrutinised.

TE 21
10 Unions must give employers seven days notice of their intention to hold a strike ballot, and seven days notice of the industrial action intended.

TE 22
11 Any individual whose goods or services are harmed by unlawful industrial action can apply for a court order to stop it.

Wages Councils

TE 35
12 These are abolished.

INTRODUCTION

In 1993 the UK Government passed probably the most significant and wide ranging employment Act since 1975. The Trade Union Reform and Employment Rights Act 1993 represents a watershed in UK employment legislation. Although parts of it, especially those dealing with trade unions and with industrial action, reinforced government policies of the 1980s, the most important provisions were introduced so as to implement European Community (EU) law or as a response to EU case law.

Some major provisions affecting employment contract documentation, the procedure for dealing with collective redundancies, aspects of business changes and transfers, maternity rights, the application of disciplinary procedures where health and safety concerns are at stake, and some important aspects of sex discrimination were legislated on. For the first time a major employment statute implemented several European Directives at once and considerably increased statutory protections for employees. The 1980s had seen some deregulation of employment relationships, coupled with an emphasis on those aspects of statutes, especially relating to job security and anti-discrimination laws, which require effective and well-managed workplace procedures. By contrast, the Trade Union Reform and Employment Rights Act 1993 marked important developments in legal protections, but also their extension to hitherto neglected groups, such as many part-timers and temporary workers.

This process increased awareness of contrasts between statutory protections in the UK and those available in other parts of the European Union.

The EU: contrasts and commonalities

As well as differences in legal systems and the enforcement and monitoring of employment law, there are some important contrasts, as well as similarities, between law and practice in the UK and other member states.

The contrasts relate generally to:

- Pay – all others have statutory regulation affecting many groups, the UK has none;
- working hours and holidays – all have laws, the UK has no basic entitlement;
- labour use strategies – some limit managerial discretion, the UK encourages sub-contracting etc.
- collective agreements and their role in the contract of employment – generally more significant outside the UK;
- worker participation – often formalised, in the UK practices vary considerably and are often more informal.

The similarities emerge over:

- Content of employment contracts;
- job security;
- the approach to occupational protections;
- law relating to equal opportunities.

Law-making in the EU

In 1972 the UK passed the European Communities Act, stating that UK law and UK courts/tribunals are required to give effect to all EU legislation and decisions of the European Court of Justice (ECJ). All UK law must be commensurate with EU law and all courts/tribunals must act consistently with the ECJ.

The law-making mechanisms

The European Commission, Director Generalite Five (DGV) develops ideas for law, following consultation with various interest groups and, usually, research exercises. Proposals for law are debated in the European Parliament which has the power to suggest, but not demand, amendments. After this process the proposed law is adopted by the Council of Ministers (for these purposes it will comprise employment ministers) usually on a qualified majority vote. This process prevents one or two countries vetoing proposals for legislation.

The legal instruments

Type	Impact on employers
(a) Articles and Regulations of The Treaty of Rome and subsequent treaties	Binding on all employers immediately. Examples of Articles are: • Art 119 (equal pay for men and women) • Art 48 (freedom of movement for EC workers) • Art 85 (prohibition of anti-competitive policies)
(b) Directives	Binding on public sector employers immediately passed; binding on private sector following UK response to ensure UK law in line with Directives. *Examples:* • Hazardous Agents Directive (1983) • COSHH Regulations (1988) • Health and Safety Framework Directive (1989)

H & S General Management Regs (1992)
- Acquired Rights Directive (1977)
Transfer of Undertakings Regs (1981)

(c) Recommendations   Highly persuasive on employers and ought not to be ignored.

Examples are:

- Recommendation on Dignity at Work (1991)
- Recommendation on Child Care (1991)

In addition there are Codes of Practice, Guidance Notes which offer advice.

Enforcement   Commission initiates action in the ECJ. National courts enforce Articles, Regulations and, of course, legislation implementing Directives.

Status of law

Although EU law is, broadly, superior to UK law where they cover the same topics the different legal instruments carry different weight. Articles are binding on all employers immediately; directives are binding on governments and the public sector and are strongly influential in all relevant case law; recommendations are strongly evidential.

Some key areas of EU law

There have been some topics of EU legislation which have been well developed, especially those given priority in the Social Charter, accepted by all EU members other than the UK.

The content of the Social Charter is:

- The freedom of movement for workers and self-employed persons across the EU;
- adequate protections for employment and remuneration;
- improvement of living and working conditions;
- adequate social protection, ie social security;
- freedom of association, ie the right to join trade unions and associations;
- adequate vocational training;
- equal treatment for men and women;
- information, consultation and participation of workers on key workplace issues;
- health protection at work;
- protection of children and adolescents at work;
- that elderly persons have adequate access to labour markets;
- that disabled persons have adequate access to labour markets.

The major topics for legislation have been:

1 *Anti-discrimination laws.* Important here are Article 119 of the Treaty of Rome (equal pay for equal work, and the Equal Treatment Directives, for example, of 1990 and 1979 (1979/7 EEC) which requires fast treatment of men and women at work.
2 *Health and safety measures.* These have rapidly developed and include directives on dangerous substances, including asbestos, safety signs, management, work equipment, work premises, noise, maternity, and the protection of other vulnerable groups at work such as the young and those with disabilities.
3 *Freedom of movement.* A series of measures have aimed to ensure that there are no significant barriers to workers obtaining work and being treated fairly in another member state. Laws cover freedom of movement itself (Art 48) and proposals to protect those seconded to another state and the mutual recognition of professional and other qualifications.

Some thoughts when using this book

Many of the topics covered by employment legislation set out in this book are well established, such as unfair dismissal, and have been subject to relatively little change in recent years. Some are long-established – for example, the requirement to provide written information about terms of work – but have been subject to significant amendment due to EU law. Other areas, such as the legal regulation of trade unions and their relationship with members, have a long history of regulation but have recently been subject to increasingly detailed provisions. A few topics are new, but mostly recent changes have modified existing rights or extended rights to more people.

Most of UK employment legislation remains dominated by UK based policies. However, with the increasing significance of EU law a qualitative change has come over law. Any UK industrial tribunal or court when applying UK legislation – itself passed so as to comply with the demands of EU law (changes to contract document collective redundancies procedures, maternity protections, for example) – must be interpreted so as to reflect fully the policy objectives. There is an increasing need for these policy objectives to be understood by practitioners, as they have very real effect on workplace policies and practices.

Professor Patricia Leighton

PART I: INDIVIDUAL RIGHTS

The Employment Protection (Consolidation) Act 1978

The Transfer of Undertakings (Protection of Employment) Regulations 1981

The Employment Acts 1980, 1989 and 1990

The Trade Union and Labour Relations (Consolidation) Act 1992

The Trade Union Reform and Employment Rights Act 1993

The Sunday Trading Act 1994

Part-time Employees (Employment Protection) Regulations 1995

WRITTEN INFORMATION TO BE SUPPLIED BY EMPLOYERS

Written particulars of terms of employment

EPC 1–6
TE Sch 4
PT

Not later than two months after starting work, every employee must receive from the employer a written statement giving.

(a) the name of the employer and the employee;
(b) the date when the employment began, taking account of any period of employment with a previous employer which counts as continuous with the present one;
(c) pay or the method of calculating it, and payment interval;
(d) any terms and conditions relating to hours of work;
(e) holiday entitlement, including public holidays and holiday pay;
(f) job title or brief description of job;
(g) place of work, or places along with the employer's address.

These make up the principal statement and must be contained in one document. In addition the following information must be given, although full details can be provided in other documents so long as these are reasonably accessible to the employee:

(h) terms and conditions relating to sickness, injury and sick pay, and to pensions;
(i) the length of notice the employee must give and receive;
(j) the period of employment if it is temporary;
(k) particulars of any collective agreements which directly affect the terms and conditions of the employment;

Comment   *Existing employees can ask their employer for the written state-*
ment of particulars of employment, and must be given it within
two months of their request. Contracts for less than one month
are exempted.

The written statement is not the same as a written contract of
employment, since it is not legally binding, as is the case with a
written contract. No signatures are required by the Act, but if an
employee is asked to sign, it should be made clear that this is
only an indication of receipt of the statement.

However accurate, clear and comprehensive the written state-
ment, there is no guarantee that the employee will understand it
properly unless it is explained verbally. The main terms and
conditions of employment ((a) to (g) opposite) should of course be
explained at the time of the interview, but will need further
clarification when employment commences work, along with an
explanation of rules and procedures ((m) over) and an opportun-
ity to ask questions.

The information about holidays should be sufficiently clear to
enable the employee to calculate precisely the entitlement to holi-
days and holiday pay, including any entitlement to accrued holi-
day pay on termination of employment.

The documents likely to be used for further reference are works
handbooks, works rules, collective agreements, booklets about
pension schemes, holiday notices. Employees need to know exac-
tly where these are kept and when they can inspect them during
working hours.

(l)   additional details of dates, currency used, special benefits and conditions of return, when the employee is to work outside the UK for more than a month;

(m) any disciplinary rules applicable to the employee, and the person to whom employees can apply if dissatisfied with a disciplinary decision or if they have a grievance about their employment, and the procedure to be followed;

(n) whether a contracting-out certificate, under the state pension scheme, is in force.

Any change to the written particulars must be notified in writing to employees individually within a month of the change.

Employers with fewer than 20 employees are exempt from (m) and (n) above except that they must specify the person to be approached over grievances: and (m) does not apply to rules and procedures governing health and safety.

EPC II   If there is any dispute about the written statement, the employer or employee may refer the matter to an industrial tribunal.

Itemised pay statement

EPC 8
TE 27
PT   At or before the time when payment of wages or salary takes place, an employee is entitled to receive from the employer an itemised pay statement, except in firms with fewer than 20 employees: in these the employee must work for five years to qualify.

The statement must show:

(a) the gross amount of the wages or salary;

A contracting-out certificate ((n) opposite) indicates that although employees may be excluded from a proportion of benefit under the State pension scheme, they will get equal or greater benefits from the employer's own pension arrangements.

Guidance on disciplinary rules and procedures is given in the ACAS advisory handbook, Discipline at Work (see page 133). This emphasises the need for management to involve employees and recognised trade unions when rules and procedure are introduced or revised, and the need for grievances to be settled fairly and promptly. The aim of the procedure should be to settle the grievance fairly and as near as possible to the point of origin. It is important that the immediate supervisor has the authority to deal with as many types of grievance as possible.

To avoid unnecessary friction and confusion, pay statements should not merely comply with the legal requirement. They should also be presented in a way that is easily understood.

(b) the amount of any fixed and variable deductions and the purposes for which they are made;

(c) the net amount of wages or salary payable;

(d) where different parts of the net amount are paid in different ways, the amount and method of payment of each part.

EPC 9

The fixed deductions can be shown as a total, without any explanation, if the employee has been given a standing statement of fixed deductions which is re-issued every 12 months.

TE 27
EPC 141

Employees who work less than eight hours a week and those who normally work abroad are excluded.

Employees or employers can refer matters related to a pay statement to an industrial tribunal. If employers have failed to show deductions, they can be ordered to pay the employee a sum based on the amount of the deductions not notified (up to a limit of 13 weeks).

Written statement of reasons for dismissal

EPC 53
4E 15
PT

An employee with at least two years' continuous service is entitled to obtain from the employer, within 14 days of making a request, a written statement of the reasons for the dismissal, and this statement will be admissible as evidence before an industrial tribunal.

The same classes of employee are excluded as for unfair dismissal (see page 54), except that the written statement provisions apply regardless of age and in the case of maternity dismissals, they apply regardless of length of service (see page 44).

An employee can complain to an industrial tribunal if the employer refuses to supply a statement or gives reasons which are inadequate or appear to be untrue. Where the

Comment   *The annual statement of fixed deductions must show the amount of each deduction, the intervals at which the deduction is to be made and the purpose for which it is made. It need not be re-issued in full each time a change is made, as long as the change is notified in writing to the employee and as long as the full statement is given to the employee at least every 12 months.*

A complaint to a tribunal over which items should have been included in a pay statement cannot be made about a job which ended more than three months previously.

Except in cases where a woman is dismissed while pregnant or on maternity leave, an employer is not obliged to provide a written statement of reasons for dismissal unless the employee has made a definite request for it. This right re-emphasises the need for a sound dismissals procedure which makes clear what are acceptable reasons for dismissal, who had the authority to dismiss, and who prepares the written statement.

It is important not only that records are kept of events leading to a dismissal, but also that the written statement is prepared at the time of the dismissal, whether or not it is requested immediately, as it might be needed months later. Vague reasons such as 'misconduct' will not suffice: they should be substantiated. The Government has said that these statements will be protected against libel actions so long as they are written in good faith. Except for those dismissed while pregnant, employees have no right to this written statement unless they ask for one.

complaint is well-founded the employer will have to pay the employee the equivalent of two weeks' pay, regardless of whether the dismissal is fair or unfair. In addition the tribunal may announce what it considers to be the reason for dismissal.

EPC 102   Written explanation of redundancy pay

On making a redundancy payment the employer must give the employee a written statement indicating how the amount of the payment has been calculated. This does not apply where a tribunal has made an award specifying the amount of redundancy payment due.

An employer who without reasonable excuse fails to provide a written statement may be fined up to £20.

If a written statement is not given, an employee may make a written request to the employer to provide it within a stated period of not less than a week. And if the employer does not do so a fine may be imposed up to £20 for a first offence and up to £100 for any further offence.

Comment   *The EAT has held that the statement should be in such a form that the reasons for dismissal are clear without reference to other documents, although a later decision of the Court of Appeal suggests that reference to other documents is in order as long as copies of them are given to the employee at the same time as the statement.*

It is preferable to give the employee the explanation of redundancy payment before the payment is made so that there is time to deal with any queries. There are three other situations arising from redundancy in which the employer has to give a written statement to the employee:

(a) *where a redundant employee wants to leave before the notice period expires and the employer objects (see page 70)*
(b) *where the trial period in a new job lasts longer than four weeks (see page 70)*
(c) *where a redundant employee goes on strike during the period of notice and the employer wants the employee to work out the notice period after the strike (see page 73).*

WAGE PAYMENT

Methods of payment

WA 11   The Wages Act 1986 repealed the Truck Acts of 1831–1860 which imposed restrictions on the way wages could be paid and, in particular, required manual workers to be paid in 'coin of the realm'.

Deductions from wages

WA 1   Deductions from wages are unlawful unless they are:

- required by law (for example national insurance, PAYE);
- provided for in the in the worker's contract of employment, so long as he has been given written details beforehand;
- agreed to in advance by the worker, in writing.

The same conditions apply where a worker has to make payment to his employer.

The exceptions to these requirements are those cases where the deduction is made (or payment received) for the following reasons:

- to recover an overpayment of wages or expenses;
- as a result of disciplinary proceedings arising from legislation;
- because the worker has taken part in a strike or other industrial action;
- to satisfy a court order or tribunal decision (though a worker must give prior consent in writing for a deduction to be made);

Comment   *Although the statutory right to insist on payment in cash no longer exists, there is nothing to prevent an employer continuing cash payment, providing the employees agree. The method of paying wages is now a matter of agreement between employer and employee.*

The Truck Acts gave some protection against unfair deductions but allowed fines to be imposed in certain circumstances – a distinction which led to much legal argument. The Wages Act makes no distinction between fines and any other kind of deduction. People who ordinarily work outside Great Britain are not covered by its provisions.

The term 'wages' is defined as any sums payable to the worker by his employer in connection with his employment, and includes such items as fees, bonuses, commission, holiday pay, statutory sick pay, guarantee payments, payments for time off, and maternity pay. It does not include loans, wage advances, pensions, or redundancy payments.

If a worker receives less money than what is due, or there is a complete non-payment, the amount of the deficit is treated as a deduction unless it arises from the employer's error in calculating the gross amount of wages. The worker is entitled to receive in full the amount unlawfully deducted following a successful complaint to an industrial tribunal.

- to meet a statutory requirement to pay specified amounts to a statutory authority;
- because of an arrangement, agreed to by the worker in writing, for the employer to make payment to a third party.

Extra protection is given in retail employment. Here deductions to cover cash or stock shortages (or payments to meet them) may not exceed one-tenth of wages on any payday, except for a final wage payment, on which there is no limit. The deductions or payments cannot start later than 12 months after the shortage comes to light.

New provisions regulating check-off arrangements for collecting union dues were introduced in the 1993 Act, in order that workers should not 'suffer deduction of unauthorised or excessive union subscriptions' (see page 94).

A worker can apply to an industrial tribunal if he or she thinks an unlawful or excessive deduction of payment has been made, and the tribunal may order reimbursement of the amount involved.

Guarantee payments

EPC 12, 13
EPC 143

In the event of short-time working, the 1978 Act provides for guarantee payments to be made to employees with at least one month's continuous service. If employees are not provided with work on a normal working day they will be entitled to a payment from their employer based on their normal daily pay, but not exceeding £14.10 a day and not exceeding five days in any period of three months. A day is defined as the period of 24 hours from midnight to midnight and the three month period is calculated up to the day of lay-off. If the days of the lay-off are not consecutive, the three month period must be calculated separately for each day.

EPC 15
E 14

Comment

'Retail employment' covers the sale or supply of goods or services (including financial services), whether on a regular basis or not; it includes workers such as cashiers and rent collectors who, though not directly involved in the sale or transaction, receive the money arising from it.

A claim arising from an unlawful deduction might also involve a failure of the employer to notify deductions, as required under EPC(A) (see pages 24 and 26). If so, a tribunal cannot make an award which exceeds the value of the deduction – the money cannot be recovered twice.

The amount of the guaranteed payment for any day is the guaranteed hourly rate times the normal number of working hours in the day up to a maximum of £14.10. And the guaranteed hourly rate is one week's pay divided by the normal working hours in a week. 'Normal working hours' do not include overtime unless it is obligatory under the employee's contract of employment.

A week's pay is defined in Schedule 14 of EP(C) A as follows:

(a) For those workers whose pay does not vary from week to week, it is the weekly pay for 'normal working hours' (see above), including any regular bonus or allowance which does not vary with the amount of work done.

33

EPC 16   Employees who are also entitled to guaranteed wages under a company scheme will receive whichever terms are better.

EPC 13   Employees forfeit their entitlement if:

(a) they have refused alternative work which is suitable in all the circumstances (even though outside the terms of their contract); or

(b) they do not comply with reasonable requirements as to their availability; or

(c) the failure to provide work is due to a strike, lock-out or other industrial action involving any employees of the same employer or of an 'associated employer' (see opposite).

The following are excluded from the scheme:

● temporary employees, that is those under contract for three months or less

● employees who normally work abroad.

If an employer fails to pay the appropriate amount, the employee can make a complaint to an industrial tribunal which can order payment to be made.

The Minister can exempt from the scheme employees who are covered by a collective agreement if it provides satisfactory arrangements for guaranteed pay and includes a right of appeal to an independent referee or to an industrial tribunal over failure to pay.

Comment

(b) *For employees whose pay varies, eg with output or with different shifts, it is the pay for the number of 'normal working hours' per week at the average hourly rate, which is calculated on the basis of hours worked and payment received during the preceding 12 weeks (including overtime hours but excluding overtime premiums.) Any week in which employees did not work at all should be replaced by the last previous week when they did.*

(c) *For employees who have not worked long enough to take account of 12 weeks, it is an amount which fairly represents a week's pay.*

The guarantee applies only if a complete working day is lost. It does not apply when an employee is sent home through lack of work after working part of the day or shift, but in such cases a redundancy payment might be claimed on the grounds of short-time working (see page 72).

The suspension of the guarantee because of industrial action applies only if the action involves employees within the firm or employees of an 'associated employer'. It cannot be suspended merely because the dispute is at a firm federated to the same employers' association.

Many company schemes for guaranteed pay are more generous than the Act in their overall effect. Nevertheless, if they are not as favourable in every respect, the two schemes must be run in parallel.

Any two employers are treated as associated if one is a company of which the other has control, or if both are companies of which a third person has control.

35

Employer's insolvency

EPC 121,
122
4E 18, 19

If an employer becomes insolvent, employees who have lost their jobs are able to claim from the National Insurance Fund debts owing to them, including arrears of pay and holiday pay; unfair dismissal basic award; guarantee and medical suspension payments; maternity pay; payment for time off; protective awards and pay in lieu of notice. In cases where the amount of money due related to a period of time, a maximum of eight weeks' pay is the general rule (six weeks for holiday pay), and in all such cases there is a limit of £205 in respect

EPC 193

of any one week. Contributions to an occupational pension fund which were unpaid at the time the employer became insolvent may also be paid from the National Insurance Fund. Employees who normally work abroad are excluded from the provision.

A person who is unsuccessful in an application for these payments can make a complaint to an industrial tribunal which can declare how much is to be paid.

Wages councils

TE 35

Part II of the Wages Act 1986 has been repealed, thereby abolishing the remaining 26 wages councils.

Comment   *Each year employees are caught up in company liquidation or bankruptcy: even when they are able to recover some of the money owing to them, the process can take years. The Act's insolvency provisions guarantee reasonably prompt payment of claims without damage to the interests of other creditors.*

An employee wishing to make a claim has to apply to the employer's representative — for example the receiver, liquidator, or trustee. Application can be made to the Employment Department if there is no representative or if payment has not been made after six months from the date of the original application.

Payment in lieu of notice is based on the statutory minimum periods of notice (see page 52).

A protective award is made for failure to consult trade union representatives about redundancies (see page 114).

The Wages Council system developed from the Trade Boards, which were established in 1909 to protect unorganised workers and to promote collective bargaining. Originally the Councils fixed varying minimum wage rates and conditions in trades where a large proportion of the employees are women and ethnic minorities, many of them part-time workers. In 1986 changes were introduced to simplify the system. At the same time a number of Councils were abolished. Their complete abolition reflects the Government attitude that minimum national statutory rates of pay have no relevance in the 1990s.

MATERNITY RIGHTS

All female employees have the rights connected with pregnancy and maternity described in the following pages. If an employer fails to grant these rights the employee affected can complain to an industrial tribunal.

General right to maternity leave

TE 23   Regardless of her length of service and hours worked, an employee is entitled to 14 weeks' maternity leave. She can choose to begin the period of leave at any time during the 11 weeks before the expected week of childbirth. The exceptions to this are:

- The maternity leave period will start sooner than the date chosen if the employee has to be absent because of pregnancy during the six weeks before the expected week of confinement.
- The maternity leave period can continue until the birth if this occurs after the end of the 14 week period.
- If, on maternity grounds, a woman is prohibited by statutory provision from working (eg because of particular health hazards) and the prohibition extends beyond the 14 weeks, the maternity leave period must be extended accordingly.
- If a woman is fairly dismissed during her period of leave, her entitlement to the full 14 weeks ends.

A woman is not necessarily required to work up until the eleventh week before confinement, but earlier absence does not count as "the maternity leave period' and does not attract the rights and benefits.

Comment   *The 1993 Act makes fundamental changes to women's preg-nancy rights, following the adoption by this country of the EU Directive in 1992. The biggest change is the introduction of the right of all women, regardless of their length of service or the hours they work, to a minimum of 14 weeks' maternity leave, during which the contract remains in existance, though the right to renumeration is suspended.*

The provisions governing the new basic period of maternity leave are less complex than those governing the longer period, which depends on length of service (see overleaf). There is some flexibility over when a woman can begin her leave.

The statutory provisions remain complex and uncertain, espec-ially regarding the legal position at the end of the 14 week period. There is no statutory right to return to work (see over) unless the woman has 2 years continuous service. However should the employer refuse her request to return, this could amount to dismissal for a reason connected with pregnancy (s24). At the time of writing, case law is pending on this and several other issues.

To qualify for this basic maternity leave an employee must:

(a) at least 21 days before her absence, or as soon as practicable, notify her employer in writing of her pregnancy, giving the date of the start of her leave and the expected week of the birth;

(b) produce a certificate from a doctor or midwife stating the expected week of childbirth if her employer asks for it.

During the period of maternity leave the same terms and conditions of employment must be maintained as if she were not absent (except for remuneration).

Those with less than two years service do not have a right to return to work.

Right of those with two years' service

TE Sch 2 The already existing right to a longer maternity absence is preserved for women with two years' or more service. They can return to work at any time up to 29 weeks after the beginning of the week in which they give birth, on the following conditions:

(a) In addition to providing the information about her pregnancy shown at (a) above, the employee must include notice to her employer that she intends to return to work.

(b) At least 21 days beforehand she must give written notice to her employer of her proposed date of return, which may not be later than 29 weeks after the actual week of childbirth.

Comment

Where redundancy (ie disappearance of the work) is the reason for not giving a woman her previous job back, employers have a duty to check whether there is a suitable vacancy, not only in their own organisation, but also with an 'associated employer' (see page 35). If there is no such vacancy she cannot claim to have been unfairly dismissed, though she can claim redundancy pay if she has the necessary service since the age of 18.

Statutory maternity pay (SMP), which depends on length of service, was introduced by the Social Security Act 1986. It is, at the time of writing, payable for a maximum of 18 weeks and cannot start earlier than the 11th week before the expected week of confinement, unless the employee has been confined before then. To get the full 18 weeks the employee must have given up work by the sixth week before the expected week of confinement.

There are two rates of pay, depending on length of service at the fifteenth week before the expected week of confinement:

- *for those with at least 26 weeks' continuous service, a set amount (currently £52.50 a week) which is reviewed each year, and is paid throughout the maternity pay period to an employee who qualifies only for this lower rate.*

(c) She must give further written confirmation of her intention to return if her employer requests it in writing; he may not do so earlier than 21 days before the end of her leave period, and she must reply within 14 days of getting the request or as soon as is reasonably practicable. (When making the request the employer must warn her that she will lose the right to return unless she replies within 14 days).

Provided the employee meets these requirements, she has the right to return to her previous job or, if this is impracticable because of redundancy, to suitable alternative work. The employer may delay her return for four weeks on giving reasons, and the employee may do the same if supported by a medical certificate.

A small firm with five or fewer employees does not have to take the employee back after the period of maternity absence if it is not reasonably practicable to do so.

As far as both types of leave are concerned, a woman who has corresponding rights under her own contract and under the Act, can opt for whichever is more favourable in any particular respect.

Time off for antenatal care

EPC 31A   A pregnant woman is entitled to time off with pay for antenatal care. Except where an antenatal appointment is the first in a pregnancy, she must produce a medical certificate confirming that she is pregnant, plus an appointment card or similar evidence, if her employer asks for them.

Comment   • *for those with at least two years' continuous service $\frac{9}{10}$ of average weekly earnings for the first six weeks, followed by up to 12 weeks at the lower rate.*

The employer is responsible for paying SMP to eligible employees but can recover some of the money by deductions from his payments of National Insurance contributions.

An employer is obliged to keep records of the following:

(a) the dates of maternity absence notified by the employee;
(b) any weeks during the maternity period for which SMP was not given, with the reasons;
(c) the medical evidence (eg maternity certificate) produced by the employee;
(d) copies of (c) where the originals have been returned to the employee.

The DSS has produced a form which can be used for keeping the necessary records – SMP2, available from social security offices.

When a woman intends to return to work after pregnancy, her employer would be well advised to discuss with her, before her departure, any problems connected with her return. She may, for example, need to change her working hours.

Where payment for antenatal time off needs to be based on the preceding 12 weeks, but the employee has not been employed that long, 'normal working hours' are the average number of hours which she herself could normally expect to work, or which are worked by others in comparable employment. The intention is that she should neither lose nor gain financially because of her time off. As well as visits to doctors, clinics etc, antenatal care is intended to cover activities such as the relaxation classes run by the National Childbirth Trust.

Payment is for the period of absence, at an hourly rate based on one week's pay divided by the normal working hours in a week. The calculation is similar to that for guarantee payments on pages 32 and 33.

Dismissal on grounds of pregnancy

TE 24
EPC 60

Regardless of her length of service or hours worked, it is unfair:

(a) to dismiss a woman for any reason connected with pregnancy or childbirth. Such a dismissal is still unfair if it occurs up to four weeks after the end of her maternity leave period, provided she is covered by a doctor's certificate stating that she is not fit to return to work.
(b) to dismiss a woman as redundant at the end of her maternity leave if she has not been offered alternative employment when there is a suitable vacancy.
(c) to dismiss a woman at the end of her maternity leave because she had taken that leave.

If an employee is dismissed while pregnant, or during her maternity leave period, she is automatically entitled to a written statement of the reasons for her dismissal without having to ask for it (see page 26).

Suspension on maternity grounds

TE Sch 3

If, due to requirements in certain health and safety regulations, an employee has to be suspended because she is pregnant, or has recently given birth, or is breastfeeding, then she has the right to be paid by her employer. She must first be offered suitable alternative work where this is available, and if she refuses this she loses her right to pay.

Comment

Where a woman is unable to do her own job, the employer is obliged to offer her a suitable alternative vacancy if there is one available; otherwise her dismissal is unfair and the employer may therefore be liable for compensation. The alternative vacancy must be one whose terms and conditions are not substantially less favourable than those of her previous job. It need not necessarily be in the same location as long as it is 'suitable'. If she refuses an offer of suitable alternative work, she is regarded as having resigned and loses her rights.

The major change in dismissal rights of pregnant women is that a claim of unfair dismissal no longer requires a two-year service qualification. This requirement had previously been challenged on the ground of unlawful sex discrimination, and for that no qualifying period is necessary.

The amount of pay in cases of suspension is a week's pay (see pages 33 and 35) for each week of suspension, and pro rata for any part of a week. The intention is for the woman to receive what she would have received had she not been suspended. Any payment made by the employer under the individual's contract will go towards discharging the employer's statutory liability, and conversely any payment under the Act will go towards discharging the employer's contractual obligations.

A woman should be told of her pregnancy rights as early as possible, particularly of the conditions governing pregnancy, dismissal, maternity pay and return to work. By resigning prematurely instead of allowing herself to be dismissed, or by failing to give written notice of her proposed absence, she could forfeit her rights.

45

TIME OFF RIGHTS

Trade union duties and activities

There are two ways in which employers are required to give reasonable time off to employees who belong to an independent trade union they 'recognise' (see pages 100 and 101):

T168–9 (a) To officials of such a union (including shop stewards) in order to carry out duties concerned with negotiations on any of the matters listed on page 118 in respect of which the employer recognises the union, or duties concerned with related matters agreed to by the employer. In addition, the Act specifically includes time spent on training for these duties. The employer must pay for time off of this kind on the basis of average hourly earnings.

T170 (b) To members of such a union in order to take part in union activities, excluding industrial action. Payment is not stipulated.

Public duties

EPC29 P An employer is required to allow reasonable time off for employees to carry out public duties. This applies to justices of the peace and members of local authorities, statutory tribunals, health authorities, water authorities, boards of prison visitors, and the governing bodies of local authority educational establishments, grant maintained schools and higher
PT education corporations. Payment is not stipulated.

Comment   *A definition of 'official' is given on page 84.*

Before 1989 the provision for time off with pay for a union official was broader, covering the carrying out of those duties 'concerned with industrial relations between his employer and any associated employer, and their employees'. It is now limited to negotiations on specific matters and, with the employer's agreement, to related matters outside the scope of negotiations. Associated employers are no longer included. By contrast, the definition of union activities – (b) opposite – is not restricted to relations with the specific employer.

Any training in industrial relations duties for which time off is allowed must have the approval of the TUC or of the official's own union. The payment for time off for industrial relations duties (unlike other payments under the Act) is based on actual remuneration, including overtime, for the period the employee would ordinarily have worked; if remuneration varies with the amount of work done, payment is based on average hourly earnings and includes overtime if normally worked.

The Code of Practice on Time Off for Trade Union Duties and Activities was revised in 1991. It gives examples of the kind of duties for which union officials might seek time off with pay: preparing for negotiations, informing members of progress, explaining the outcome to them. Activities for which union members might be given unpaid time off could include: attending workplace meetings to discuss the outcome of negotiations, meeting full-time officials to discuss workplace issues, voting in ballots.

Arrangements for handling time off appropriate to the particular situation can usefully be embodied in agreements. Subjects for attention could include the method of identifying the union officials affected and their constituencies; the duties and activities involved, including any which arise regularly; the position of officials in minority unions; the time needed for training; whether existing procedures are adequate for dealing with disputes over time off; a system of control.

Looking for work

EPC31   Employees with at least two years' continuous service who have been declared redundant must, before their notice expires, be allowed reasonable time off to look for new employment. They must be paid at their hourly rate.

Suspension on medical grounds

EPC19   Some processes are covered by special health and safety regulations under which employees may be suspended from their normal work because of health hazards (see opposite). In such cases employees who are suspended on medical grounds may be entitled to receive payment from their employer provided they have at least one month's continuous service.

EPC21   The amount will be a week's pay (see pages 33 and 35) for every week of suspension up to a maximum of 26 weeks. Employees who are entitled under their contract of employment to payment during medical suspension, will receive whichever terms are better.

EPC20   Employees will forfeit their entitlement if:

(a) they unreasonably refuse an offer from their employer of suitable alternative work; or
(b) they do not comply with reasonable requirements as to their availability; or
(c) they are incapable of work because of sickness or injury.

The following are not entitled to this payment:

Comment   *Although a tribunal award for time off to look for work is limited to two-fifths of a week's pay, this does not mean that the time off is so limited. The governing word is 'reasonable'.*

Safety representatives, appointed by recognised independent unions under the Health and Safety at Work Act, are entitled to time off with pay to carry out their functions and to undergo training. (See the Safety Representatives and Safety Committees Regulations 1977 and the Code of Practice on the subject).

This part of the Employment Protection (Consolidation) Act 1978 applies only if the provision is specified in its Schedule 1, or is required by a Code of Practice approved by the Health and Safety Commission. The following Regulations are involved:

- *The Control of Lead at Work Regulations 1980*
- *The Ionizing Radiation Regulations 1985*
- *The Control of Substances Hazardous to Health Regulations 1988, Reg 11.*

The original list of Regulations in Schedule 1 of EP(C) A was longer, but later Orders have consolidated a number of them.

As with guarantee payments, the entitlement is forfeited if the employee refuses to do suitable alternative work, and this includes work which is outside the employee's normal contract.

49

- temporary employees, that is those under contract for three months or less
- employees who normally work abroad.

EPC61(2) Replacement employees can be fairly dismissed because of the return of the suspended employee provided they were informed in writing on engagement that this would happen, and provided the employer acted reasonably over the dismissal.

EPC64(2) If the employees are dismissed when they should have been given medical suspension, they can claim unfair dismissal provided they have at least four weeks' service (compared with two years which is now the normal qualifying period for unfair dismissal).

Maternity

Time off for antenatal care is dealt with on page 42, and suspension on maternity grounds on page 44.

Infringement of time off right

EPC 22
T172 If employees are refused time off, or if they are not properly paid for it, they can complain to an industrial tribunal which may award compensation.

Sunday Working

ST4
Sched 4 Under the Sunday Trading Act 1994, an employee who complies with certain procedures cannot be required to work on a Sunday. An employee who is a 'protected shop worker' can claim for unfair dismissal in the event of being dismissed for refusing to work on a Sunday.

Comment   *The provisions relating to employment protection were added to the Sunday Trading Act as a consequence of deregulation of shop opening hours. The Act applies to the retail trade, including services, and covers all employees other than those employed solely to work on a Sunday.*

An employee cannot be required to work on a Sunday if that person is either:

(a) A 'protected shop worker', i.e. an employee whose employment contract as a shop worker cannot require Sunday working, or

(b) an 'opted-out' shop worker, i.e. has served an opting-out notice on his employer three months previously. Reasons for opting out do not have to be given.

An employee can also 'opt-in', i.e. agree to work on Sundays.

Dismissal for refusal to work on Sunday is deemed to be for an automatically unfair reason. Claims can also be made if an employee suffers a 'detriment' − e.g. is not promoted, has a bonus witheld − and compensation can be awarded by an industrial tribunal.

Both opting-in and opting-out notices have to require with statutory wording set out in the Act itself.

PERIODS OF NOTICE

EPC 49   An employee is entitled to the following notice from the employer:

(a) one week after one month's continuous employment
(b) one week for each year of continuous employment between two and 12 years
(c) twelve weeks if the period of continuous employment is 12 years of more.

An employee is required to give the employer at least one week's notice after one month's continuous service. This does not increase with longer service.

The following are not covered by the rights to notice:

- temporary employees, that is those under a contract for three months or less
EPC 141
- employees who normally work abroad.

EPC 50   Employees who are entitled to one of the minimum periods
Sch 3   of notice set out above, but who do not work during part or all of that period, must be paid for normal working hours lost if:

- they are ready for work but none is provided; or
- they are unable to work through sickness or injury; or
- they are on holiday.

Payment is based on the average hourly rate, ie a week's pay divided by the number of normal working hours; or, where there are no normal hours, the employee is entitled to a week's pay for each week of notice, based on the average weekly pay for the preceding 12 weeks. (See the section on a week's pay, pages 33 and 35).

Comment   *The periods of notice required by the Act are minimum periods. There is nothing to prevent employer and employee agreeing longer periods. The notice provisions do not generally apply to fixed-term contracts, including apprenticeships, since employer and employee know when they are to end. But employees originally engaged under a short-term contract are entitled to a minimum period of notice if in fact they are continuously employed for three months or more. If apprentices remain with their employer after completing their apprenticeship, their period as apprentices counts when calculating the amount of notice they are entitled to.*

An employer can still dismiss an employee without notice for gross misconduct (whether the dismissal is 'unfair' or not is a separate issue) and an employee can leave without notice if the employer's behaviour justifies it.

The right to pay during notice does not apply to any time the employee is allowed off during notice at his own request, unless he is entitled to it for trade union duties or public duties, to look for work or make arrangements for training, or for antenatal care (see pages 46 to 50). Nor is an employee entitled to be paid twice for the same period, so for example the amount of notice pay may be reduced if sickness payment is being made.

Where it is necessary to calculate an average payment based on the preceding 12 weeks, but the employee has not worked that long, a week's pay is an amount 'which fairly represents a week's pay'.

To qualify for either kind of maternity leave a woman must give her employers at least 21 days' notice of the start of her leave (see page 40).

UNFAIR DISMISSAL

EPC 54   With certain exceptions, employees with at least two years' continuous service are given legal protection against unfair dismissal. The exceptions include:

EPC 64(1)
- employees who have reached the normal retiring age for their job if it is the same for men and women, or who are over 65

EPC 141
- employees who normally work abroad.

There is no qualifying period for claims of unfair dismissal arising from trade union membership or activities; pregnancy; legitimate health and safety activities; action to enforce statutory rights (see (a) (c) (d) (e) on page 56). In cases of dismissal connected with the Act's provisions on medical suspension (see page 48) the qualifying period is one month.

EPC 55(2)   An employee's resignation which is justified because of the conduct of the employer is treated as a dismissal: it is a 'constructive dismissal' (see opposite).

Fairness

EPC 57   A dismissal is **fair** if an employer has acted reasonably and has dismissed an employee for any of the following reasons:

(a) lack of capability or of appropriate qualifications
(b) misconduct
(c) redundancy
(d) contravention of statutory requirements
(e) some other substantial reason sufficient to justify the particular dismissal.

Comment   *Although the age limit for the right to complain of unfair dismissal is now the same for men and women and, as a result, occupational pensions are under examination to bring them into line, state retirement pensions are not yet affected.*

The interpretation of 'normal retiring age' depends on what happens in practice – ie, what is the reasonable expectation of the employee at the time in question.

The following are examples of the kind of conduct by an employer which could lead to a claim of 'constructive dismissal': arbitrary reduction of pay, arbitrary change of duties, hours or location, failure to observe disciplinary procedures, failure to take reasonable care for the safety of employees, insulting behaviour, social and sexual harrassment. The test is whether there has been a fundamental breach of the employment contract. A claim for unfair dismissal on these grounds is not normally possible if the employee does not resign as this implies that the breach of contract has been accepted: the resignation need not be immediate – the employee is entitled to a reasonable amount of time to decide.

An employee on a fixed-term contact, whose contract is not renewed when the term expires, is regarded as dismissed. But where the contract is for one year or more, the employee can forego the right to claim unfair dismissal at the end of it, providing he or she has agreed to this, in writing, beforehand.

'Some other substantial reason' has included, pressure from customers, disruption of staff caused by a difficult employee, false details on an application form, proven business need.

Unfairness

A dismissal is unfair if:

T152   (a) It is for belonging to, or taking part in the activities of, an 'independent union' (see page 84), or it is for refusing to join a particular union or a union of any kind or refusing
T153   to make payments in lieu of union membership; or if selection for redundancy has been on trade union grounds.

EPC 59   (b) It is in breach of an agreed or customary redundancy procedure and there are no special reasons for departing from that procedure.

EPC 60   (c) It is solely because the employee is pregnant or for any reason connected with the pregnancy, except where she is incapable of working or prohibited by statutory provisions (see page 44).

TE 28   (d) It is because the employee took steps to avoid imminent danger at work, or was carrying out recognised duties in connection with health and safety.

TE 29   (e) It is because the employee sought to uphold any statutory employment protection right, whether or not the right applied to that person.

TUPE 8   (f) It arises from the transfer of a business from one employer to another unless there are economic, technical or organisational grounds for changes in the work force;

EPC 64   (g) It is because of a woman's retirement age when a man in comparable circumstances would not be dismissed;

EPC 57   (h) Insufficient reason is shown or if the dismissal is not reasonable in the particular circumstances.

In the case of (a) (c) (d) (e) above, the right not to be unfairly dismissed applies regardless of length of service or hours worked and regardless of the size of the firm.

T238   Dismissal at the time of a strike or other industrial action, or at the time of a lock out, is not unfair if all the employees concerned are dismissed. But if, at the particular establish-

Comment   *Even though the reason for dismissal is a fair one, unfairness can arise because the employer acted unreasonably in treating it as a sufficient reason. The EAT has emphasised that industrial tribunals should take into account the principles of natural justice and of good industrial relations practice. Has the employee been informed of the allegations against him or her? Have previous warnings been given and have these made clear the consequences of a further offence? Has account been taken of such matters as the employee's length of service? In cases of redundancy the employer would be expected to be able to explain the criteria used for selecting the employees to be dismissed. A dismissal on the grounds of lack of capability to do the job would be unlikely to be regarded as fair if the employer had not provided adequate training, or explained the standards required, or given reasonable opportunity for improvement.*

Particularly important is the way in which the dismissal has been carried out, and the need to:

- *ensure that immediate superiors do not normally have the power to dismiss without reference to senior management*
- *give individuals the opportunity to state their case before a decision is reached*
- *give individuals the right to be accompanied by a trade union representative or a fellow employee of their choice*
- *ensure that, except for gross misconduct, no employees are dismissed for a first breach of discipline*
- *ensure that disciplinary action is not taken until the case has been carefully investigated*
- *ensure that individuals are given an explanation for any penalty imposed*
- *provide a right of appeal.*

Summary dismissal (ie dismissal without notice), following gross misconduct, is a particularly serious step. As far as possible disciplinary rules should indicate the type of offence which would warrant summary dismissal — examples have included smoking where there is a risk of explosion; falsification of time

ment, some of the employees still on strike are dismissed, or are not offered re-engagement within three months when others have been, they can claim unfair dismissal if the reason they have been singled out is an unfair one within the meaning of the Act. This provision, which is aimed at preventing selective dismissals in a strike, does not apply to 'unofficial' action, that is, action of trade union members which has not been authorised by the union. Individuals taking part in such action have no right to claim unfair dismissal (see page 126).

T237

Complaints to industrial tribunals

EPC 67

Individuals who consider they have been unfairly dismissed can, from the time they receive notice, complain to an industrial tribunal, (see page 134) and should do so within three months of leaving. (This time limit can be extended if not reasonably practical. In cases relating to selective re-engagement after a strike, the time limit is six months). There is then an opportunity for conciliation, at the request of either side or at the suggestion of a conciliation officer, with a view to reaching a voluntary settlement.

EPC 134

If the case goes on to the tribunal, it is for the employers to show that the reason for the dismissal was justifiable under the Act. But they no longer are obliged to show that they acted reasonably in all the circumstances. That is for the tribunal to decide.

EPC 57(3)

In determining whether or not a dismissal was fair, a tribunal must take account of the size and administrative resources of the undertaking. It must not take account of any pressure exerted on the employer to secure the dismissal, for example, by threatened strike.

E6

EPC 63

Where a union, or anyone else, has used industrial action, or the threat of it, to bring about the dismissal of a non-union

T160

Comment   *cards; violence; unauthorised entry to a computer. In such cases an employer still needs to investigate the circumstances, and a brief period of suspension with pay may be necessary while this is going on.*

Industrial action taken by a non-union workforce is not 'unofficial' for the purpose of this section of the Act; in such a case the employer would still have to dismiss all or none to avoid unfairness.

Since employees can apply to an industrial tribunal as soon as they receive notice, conciliation may be possible before they leave their job. Employees should be told of this, and of their other dismissal rights, when they are given notice. The advantage of conciliation is that it is speedy, inexpensive and informal.

Employers or employees need not wait for a conciliation officer to contact them. They can make the approach themselves through their regional ACAS office, but the employee should not on that account delay putting in an application to the tribunal since the process of conciliation does not extend the three month's time limit, nor does any delay caused by an appeal through internal machinery.

Employees wishing to take their case to an industrial tribunal can get an application form and an explanatory leaflet (ITL 1) from any local employment office or employment benefit office.

The consideration of size and resources is intended to ease the burden on small firms. In their case, dismissals are not likely to be judged unfair merely because the formal requirements of the Code on disciplinary practice and procedures (see page 105) were not observed, as long as the matter was properly investigated and dealt with fairly.

An industrial tribunal may, at the request of either side or on its own initiative, hold a pre-hearing review if it seems that one of the parties has a hopeless or unreasonable case, and that party

employee, the person responsible can be required by the employer or the employee to be a party to the proceedings, and can be ordered to pay all or part of the compensation.

T161
T162
T164
T166

Employees who think they have been dismissed for trade union membership or activity, or for non-membership of a union, can obtain a preliminary (interim) hearing from a special tribunal. They must make application within seven days of the dismissal and, where appropriate, must produce a supporting certificate from the independent union to which they belong, or hope to belong. The tribunal must give the employer seven days' notice of the hearing and, where there is time, must also notify the union or anyone else who is to be a party to the proceedings. It can order temporary reinstatement of the employee, temporary re-engagement, or suspension on full pay, pending the full hearing. And it can award compensation if its order is not carried out by the employer.

TE 39

Under the 1993 Act it became possible in certain cases to avoid tribunal proceedings by making a 'compromise agreement' (see page 135).

Reinstatement and re-engagement

EPC 69

In cases where dismissal has been found unfair and the employee is prepared to return to the previous employer, the industrial tribunal must first examine the possibility of reinstatement in the old job, and next the possibility of re-engagement in a comparable job with the same or an associated employer. The test is one of practicability.

EPC 70

The tribunal can make an order for reinstatement or re-engagement and state the terms on which this should take place. The fact that a permanent replacement has been engaged must be disregarded, unless the employer can show that the work could not be done without one, or that the original

Comment   *may be required to deposit £150 as a condition of proceeding to a full hearing.*

The purpose of the quick, interim hearing is to reduce the likelihood of industrial action in cases where employees believe that an individual has been victimised for his trade union activities or for not being a member of the union. These situations are inevitably critical and employers will no doubt choose to be present at the hearing to put their point of view at an early stage.

The significance of reinstatement, as opposed to re-engagement, is that employees are treated in all respects as if they had not been dismissed. It ensures that accrued benefits which depend on length of service are not lost, eg benefits arising under pension schemes, holiday sickness pay arrangements, and entitlement to redundancy pay. An order for re-engagement is more flexible. It usually means an order for the employee to return to a different job, but on terms which are, so far as is practicable, as favourable as an order for reinstatement.

Although orders for reinstatement and re-engagement were originally intended to be the principal remedies for unfair dismissal, they are rarely made. This is often because they are not practicable – ie, not 'capable of being carried into effect with success', as one judge put it: relationships may have broken down irrevo-

61

employee had not indicated within a reasonable time a wish to return.

Compensation

EPC 72

There are three main kinds of award payable by the employer to the employee; (a) basic; (b) compensatory; and (c) special. In addition, there is a fourth which, like the special award, is punitive and is for refusal to comply with an order for reinstatement or re-engagement in cases other than those covered by the special award. The details are as follows:

EPC 73

T156

(a) The basic award is related to length of service and is equal to the sum the employee would have received if dismissed for redundancy. It is calculated in the same way as redundancy pay except that years worked between the ages of 16 and 18 count here. Where the dismissal was because of membership or non-membership of a trade union (see (c) below) there is a minimum basic award of £2,700. Otherwise the award is based on weekly pay, with a weekly maximum of £205 and a total maximum of £6,150. The amount is reduced in respect of any redundancy payment that is made.

EPC 74
EPC75
TE 30

(b) In addition, a compensatory award can be made, based on any loss sustained by the employee as a result of dismissal, including expenses incurred, loss of earnings, loss of pension rights and any other benefits. The maximum here is £11,000.

Comment   *cably and the employee may have no wish to return. Re-employment can be particularly difficult in small firms where alternative placements and grouping are often not possible.*

The EAT has said that, before making an order for reinstatement, the industrial tribunal should decide whether it is in fact practicable. Where an employer fails to comply with a tribunal order to reinstate or re-engage employees who have been unfairly dismissed, the compensation awarded can equal the amount that would have been due had the employer complied. This is intended to remove any financial incentive not to reinstate.

A limit on compensation such as the £11,000 at (b) opposite, can be ignored when the law concerned is one generated by the European Commission – eg TUPE (see page 76) and some maternity rights (see page 39).

The 'special award' substantially increases the compensation available for those dismissed unfairly for union membership or activities or for not belonging to a union. In addition to the basic award (with its minimum £2,700 in these cases) and the compensatory award, the special award would be as follows:

(i)   *Where reinstatement is sought but no order is made by the tribunal – 104 weeks' pay, subject to a minimum of £13,400 and a maximum of £26,800.*

(ii)   *Where reinstatement is ordered by the tribunal but the order is not complied with – 156 weeks' pay, subject to a minimum of £20,100 (and no weekly maximum), unless the employer satisfies the tribunal that it was not practicable to comply, in which case the amount would be as in (i) above.*

Note
The amounts payable in compensation for unfair dismissal are periodically revised. The amounts quoted here, and elsewhere in this book were correct in March 1995.

T 157

T 158

(c) The 'special award' is for those dismissed unfairly because of non-membership of a trade union, or because of trade union membership or activities, and applies where the employee asks the tribunal for an order for reinstatement or re-engagement, whether or not such an order is made. It is additional to (a) and (b) above and ranges from a minimum of £13,400 to no maximum in certain cases (see opposite).

EPC 71
TE 30

(d) In other cases where, contrary to an order for reinstatement or re-engagement, an employer does not take back the employee when it is practicable to do so, the tribunal may in addition to (a) and (b) above award the employee a sum of between 13 and 26 week's pay (between 26 and 52 weeks' pay for sex or race discrimination). The maximum weekly pay, that can be taken into account is £205, and the maximum of £11,000 at (b) can be disregarded.

These awards may be reduced on account of the employee's conduct before dismissal, or because the employee has unreasonably prevented reinstatement or because he has failed to take reasonable steps to lessen the loss.

Exemption for approved procedures

EPC 65

Exemption from the statutory machinery can be obtained, on application to the Secretary of State, where satisfactory dismissal procedures have been established by collective agreement. Such procedures must include remedies as beneficial as those given by the Act, and must include a right to arbitration or adjudication by an independent referee or body. Exemption is available only for agreements made by independent trade unions.

A woman dismissed on the grounds of pregnancy can still complain to an industrial tribunal, even though she is

Comment   *With the introduction of such high awards it is clear that the aim is to induce employers to comply with an order of reinstatement. As a safeguard against an employee's abuse of these awards, a tribunal has the power to reduce the amount if the employee's conduct before dismissal warranted it.*

A dismissal may constitute unlawful discrimination under the Sex Discrimination Act 1975 or the Race Relations Act 1976, as well as unfair dismissal under EP(C)A. If so, the dismissed employee can make a complaint to a tribunal under two Acts, but will not receive double compensation for any particular aspect of the dismissal.

It is essential that all levels of supervision and management understand the implications of the statutory provisions on dismissal, as well as the policies and procedures of their own company. This is especially true of first-line supervisors. They are usually the people who initiate the action leading to dismissal, and they are the people who will have to take back the reinstated employee. Ample opportunity should be given to supervisors to discuss dismissal and disciplinary problems with senior management, and to have their views taken into account when policies are being formulated.

In reviewing company policy on dismissal an employer needs to pay particular attention to the following questions:

covered by an exempted agreement which makes other provisions for adjudication.

Individuals can also opt out of using the statutory machinery to some extent through 'compromise agreements' (see page 135).

● For a more detailed explanation of the subject, see *'Unfair Dismissal'* by Richard W Painter in the *Employment Law Guides* series, published by Nicholas Brealey Publishing in association with the Industrial Society.

Comment   (a) *Who in the organisation has the authority to dismiss?*

(b) *What steps are taken to ensure that those with the authority to dismiss know what is 'fair'?*

(c) *Are works/office rules clear and known to employees?*

(d) *Is there an adequate disciplinary procedure in operation?*

(e) *Are adequate records kept of all dismissals? Employers have got to be able to show good reason. If, as often happens, the dismissal is a result of deteriorating performance over a period of time, employers must be able to prove all the facts and not just the 'last straw'. Their records should include short service employees, employees above retiring age and those who work minimal hours, since although these categories are excluded from the general provisions on unfair dismissal, they can make a claim if dismissed in connection with trade union membership or non-membership, for example (see page 56).*

Detailed guidance and examples are given in the free ACAS handbook Discipline at Work *(see page 133).*

REDUNDANCY PAYMENTS

EPC 81   With certain exceptions employees with at least two years' continuous service since the age of 18, who are dismissed because of redundancy, are entitled to a lump-sum payment from their employer. The amount of payment depends on age, pay and length of service, as follows:

EPC Sch4   For each of year of continuous employment

from age 41 to 64	1.5 weeks pay
from age 22 to 40	1 weeks pay
from age 18 to 21	0.5 weeks pay

EPC Sch 14(8)   At the time of writing £205 is the maximum weekly pay that can be taken into account, and 20 years the maximum service. Thus the maximum redundancy payment possible is £6,150 (20 years service between 41 and 64, ie 30 times £205). The amount is reduced by one-twelfth for each complete month over the age of 64, so that at 65 no payment is due.

Employees laid off or kept on short time for a specified period are also entitled to redundancy payment in certain circumstances (see page 72).

EPC 102   The employer has to give the employee a written explanation of a redundancy payment (see page 102).

Employees not eligible for redundancy pay include:

EPC 82
4E16   ● employees over normal retiring age for the job if it is the same for men and women, or is over 65
EPC 141   ● employees who normally work abroad, unless at the time of their dismissal they are in this country on their employer's instructions.

Comments   *Dismissal for redundancy occurs if the dismissal is due 'wholly or mainly' to the fact that the employer requires fewer employees to carry out certain work. As well as in the obvious cases such as shut-downs of part of a business or total closures, a redundancy occurs if a reorganisation of a business means that the same work can be done by fewer people, or if the work cannot be done through lack of funds. Employees cannot automatically be treated as redundant merely because their own job has disappeared; it is necessary to show that there is no other work available which they could be required to do under their contract of employment.*

If employees are dismissed because their place is taken by another employee who was redundant elsewhere in the organisation, the dismissal is regarded as due to redundancy. This is also the case where there is no reduction in work, but a reorganisation makes the duties of a new replacement employee different from those of the one dismissed, ie there is a reduced need for work of a particular kind.

If employees have already been given notice because of redundancy, and are then dismissed for misconduct during the period of notice, they do not necessarily lose their entitlement.

As with the provisions for unfair dismissal, constructive dismissal is treated as dismissal for redundancy purposes. This would cover the case where, in order to avoid making a redundancy payment, an employer forces an employee to resign by breaking the contract of employment.

Apprentices leaving at the end of their apprenticeship would not normally be entitled to a payment since their departure would not be due to redundancy, but they might be entitled if their employer is one who usually offers employment at the end of apprenticeships and is only prevented from doing so because of redundancy.

Employees choosing voluntary redundancy or early retirement might forfeit a statutory redundancy payment, as they have not been dismissed but have apparently agreed to the termination of their employment; though where an employer has called for

EPC 142
- employees under a fixed-term contract of two years or more, who have previously agreed in writing to forgo the payment when the contract expires.

Offers of further employment

EPC 84
Employees, who have been given notice on redundancy grounds, may lose their entitlement to redundancy pay if their employer (or an 'associated employer' or a new owner of the business) offers them their old job back or another suitable job and they unreasonably refuse. Such an offer need not be in writing, but:

- it must be made before the employee's notice expires
- it must take effect immediately the previous employment ends or within four weeks
- the job must be suitable for the employee.

Where the job offered is different from the previous one, or is the same but with different conditions, the employee can give it a trial for four weeks without losing rights to redundancy payment. For the purpose of retraining the trial period can be longer if agreed in writing with the employer.

EPC 85
Employees leaving before their notice expires

Employees who have been made redundant and who want to leave before their notice is up, can themselves give notice in writing to their employer, and their entitlement to redundancy pay will not be affected, provided the employer has no objection to the earlier date of leaving. If the employer does object, and asks the employee in writing to work out the original notice, stating that otherwise the claim for redundancy pay will be contested, payment can be withheld. The employee may then apply to an industrial tribunal for a ruling whether any payment should be made.

Comment   *volunteers to accept redundancy, the resulting dismissals should warrant redundancy payments as, in such cases, it is the employer who has terminated the employment.*

Where an employee accepts an offer of further employment, as described opposite, the new work and the old count as continuous employment, and if there is a break of not more than four weeks, this too counts as a period of employment. 'Associated employer' is defined on page 35.

The Act gives no guidance on what can be regarded as 'suitable' further employment, but where there is any doubt the question can be referred to an industrial tribunal. Location, earning, skills required, fringe benefits, and prospects would be the kind of factors likely to be taken into account. Disputes about whether an employee is unreasonable in refusing a new job can also be referred to a tribunal.

As well as being in writing, an agreement about a trial period longer than four weeks must also:

- *be made before the employee starts the new job*
- *specify the date of the end of the trial period*
- *specify the terms and conditions of employment which will apply after the end of the trial period.*

A refusal to allow a trial period has been treated as constructive dismissal.

If an employee is dismissed during or at the end of the trial period because of failure to reach the standard required, the dismissal is still one of redundancy.

An employer who find alternative work for a redundant employee with another employer is not relieved of the obligation to make a payment, unless the other employer is a new owner of the business or an 'associated employer' (see page 35).

The mere change in the identity of an employer does not entitle an employee to resign and claim redundancy pay (see TUPE Regulations page 76).

Strikes during notice

EPC 110   If employees are dismissed for going on strike during the period of notice, they are still entitled to any redundancy pay which would have been due to them. However, at the request of the employer, they may have to return to work after the strike and stay for as many days as were lost through striking, even though these go beyond the original period of notice. If they do not return as requested, the employer is not obliged to make a payment but the employees are still free to apply to a tribunal for a ruling.

Lay-offs and short time

EPC 87   Employees may be entitled to a redundancy payment if they have been laid off or kept on short time:

(a) for at least four consecutive weeks, or
(b) for a broken series of at least six weeks in a 13 week period.

They cannot claim such redundancy payment unless, within four weeks of the end of the short time or lay-off periods, they have notified their employer in writing of their intention to do so. If, on receiving the notification, the employer thinks
EPC 88(4)   there is a reasonable prospect that normal working will be
EPC 89   resumed within four weeks (and last for at least 13 weeks), he can, within seven days, issue to the employee a 'counter-notice' stating that he will contest redundancy payment. payment.

EPC 89(5) Employees cannot get redundancy payment in these cases unless they have left the employment, having given their normal notice of leaving.

There is no entitlement if the lay-off or short time is due to a strike or lock-out, wherever it occurs.

Comment   *An employer's request to an employee to return to work after a strike must be in writing, must indicate why the request is being made, and must state that the employer will oppose redundancy payment unless the employee complies with the request or has good reason for not doing so.*

Appendix 2 of the ACAS booklet Redundancy Handling (see page 133) explains the redundancy payments system, including the method of calculating payment.

A week of lay-offs means a week for which employees get no pay because the employer has no work for them of the kind they are employed to do. A week of short time is a week for which employees get less than half a week's pay because of a shortage of such work. Calculation of a week's pay is explained on pages 33 and 35.

Employees entitled to a guaranteed minimum wage are not considered to be on short time (even though not working), unless the guaranteed wage is less than half a week's pay.

The employee can appeal to a tribunal against a counter-notice. If the employee continues to be laid off or kept on short time during each of the four weeks following notification to the employer, he will be entitled to payment.

The employee's notice of intention to claim a payment on account of short time, and notice of leaving the employment, are quite separate and do not have to be given at the same time. The time limits for giving notice of leaving are as follows:

(a) if the employer does not give a counter-notice, within four weeks of the employee's notification of claim

(b) if the employer gives a counter-notice but withdraws it, within three weeks of the withdrawal

(c) if the question of payment has been referred to an industrial tribunal, within three weeks of the tribunal's decision.

Making a claim

EPC
101(1)

If, soon after dismissal, employees do not receive the redundancy pay which they think is due to them, they should make a claim in writing to their employer. Should they fail to do this within six months of the date their employment ended they may lose their right to redundancy pay, unless they have already referred their claim for payment to an industrial tribunal or have made a complaint of unfair dismissal to a tribunal. Where there is a good reason for delay, a tribunal can allow employees a further six months so long as they make their claim to their employer or refer to a tribunal in that time.

EPC
101(2)

EPC 91

Any question about the right of an employee to a redundancy payment, or about the amount of payment, can be referred to an industrial tribunal for settlement.

Rebates to employers

4E 17
5E13

Up to 1989 employers with fewer than ten employees who made a redundancy payment under the Act could claim back a percentage of the cost from the Redundancy Fund. This entitlement has now been abolished as has the Redundancy Fund.

Exemption for approved schemes

EPC 96

Exemption from the statutory right to redundancy pay can be obtained, on application to the Secretary of State, for employees who are covered by an acceptable collective agreement on severance pay. Such an agreement must include provision for disputes about employees' rights to redundancy payment to be settled by an industrial tribunal.

● For further information, see '*Handling redundancy*' by Sue Morris in the *Employment Law Guides* series, published by Nicholas Brealey Publishing in association with the Industrial Society.

Comment   *The time limit for the employee to apply to an industrial tribunal on questions of redundancy payment is, in general, six months, compared with three months for unfair dismissal.*

If the employee is dissatisfied with the result of his claim to the employer, or if he was employed by somebody now dead, or if he does not receive payment from his employer within a reasonable time after a tribunal award, he should consult the nearest employment office or unemployment benefit office.

The opportunity for exemption from statutory redundancy payments is not limited to agreements made by independent trade unions as it is in the case of dismissal procedures.

The procedure for handling collective redundancies is dealt with on pages 112–17.

TRANSFER OF UNDERTAKINGS

The Transfer of Undertakings (Protection of Employment) Regulations 1981 were brought in to implement the EEC Acquired Rights Directive of 1977, and were amended by TUER (see opposite). They safeguard employee's rights when there is a change of employer following the transfer or merger of a business undertaking (commercial or otherwise).

Their effect is that:

TUPE 5   (a) The transfer of a business undertaking does not terminate the contract of employment of a person employed 'immediately before' the transfer. Instead, the contract is automatically transferred to the new employer along with *TUPE 6* related rights and obligations, including those arising out of collective agreements but not including rights to occupational pensions.

TUPE 8   (b) A dismissal is automatically unfair if the reason for it is connected with the transfer of the business, except where there are 'economic, technical or organisational' grounds for changes in the work-force, in which case the dismissal is regarded as being for 'some other substantial reason' (see page 55). This regulation on dismissal applies both to employees of the previous employer and the new one, and to those who are not transferred as well as those who are.

TUPE 9   (c) Recognition rights of independent trade unions are automatically transferred if the undertaking maintains its distinct identity.

TUPE 10 (d) Both the old and new employer must provide advance information about a proposed transfer to any independent recognised trade unions, and must consult them on any measure which will affect the employees they represent, with a view to seeking their agreement. Details of the information which must be given are to be found in

Comment   *The original 1981 Regulations did not meet all the requirements of the EEC Directive and were therefore amended by the 1993 Act. One result is that non-commercial undertakings are no longer excluded. How far this will affect, for example, the contracting out of government and local authority services has yet to be clarified, bearing in mind that the transfer of an undertaking need not entail the transfer of property. The test is whether a going concern (or a self-contained part of it) has been transferred, remaining the same business but in different hands.*

Under the Regulations the transferred employees retain all the rights and obligations existing under the old owner, apart from occupational pension rights and invalidity and survivors' benefits. Their period of continuous employment is not broken by the transfer, so the date they started work with the old owner is the starting date for calculating length of service. There have been conflicting opinions about which employees are covered – ie what is meant by those employed 'immediately before the transfer'. But a House of Lords decision has stated that it means 'employed immediately before the transfer or would have been employed had he not been unfairly dismissed in circumstances described in regulation 8(a).' It does not mean only those employees still in employment at the time of the transfer, as was once claimed.

Regulation 8 ((b) opposite) can apply to dismissals which take place some time before of after the date of the transfer, so long as the reason is not in the 'economic, technical or organisation' category. The wording here refers to dismissals 'connected with' the business transfer without stipulating a particular time.

The significance of 'some other substantial reason' for a dismissal, as the alternative in (b) opposite, is that it is not automatically regarded as unfair: it has to be judged by normal unfair dismissal rules, including that of whether the employer has acted reasonably. The phrase 'changes in the work-force' does not mean mere changes in the identity of individuals. It must involve a change in the overall number of employees or a change in their duties.

the section on Disclosure of Information (page 108).

Complaints to an industrial tribunal can be made by employees who have lost their job because of a transfer, and by trade union representatives if an employer has failed to inform and consult as required.

Comment *If an employee informs his employer that he objects to being transferred, his employment can be terminated but he will not be treated as having been dismissed.*

If, as a result of a transfer, employees find there has been a change for the worse in their terms and conditions, they can resign and make a claim for constructive dismissal (see page 54).

CONTINUITY OF EMPLOYMENT

EPC
Sched 13
PT

Many statutory rights, in particular, redundancy and unfair dismissal normally require two years continuous employment. There are no requirements for a prescribed number of weekly working hours.

Periods which count towards the two year qualifying period are any periods 'governed by a contract', including the maternity leave period (see page 38), any period of suspension, secondment or any period where the contract subsists, though the obligation to perform work is discontinued.

EPC
Sched 13
Para 9

Continuity is also prescribed in some situations where there is 'no contract of employment'.

Comment   *The two important circumstances are where the employee is:*

- *'absent from work' on account of a temporary cessation of work, or,*
- *absent from work in circumstances such that, by arrangement or custom, he is regarded as continuing in the employment of his employer for all or any purposes.*

A 'temporary cessation' has relevance to seasonal, casual and other temporary staff and will preserve continuity during a lay-off period so long as the periods in work are greater than the gaps in work and there is an understanding, borne out by work patterns, that when work is available it will be offered to the relevant worker.

The weeks that count towards a period of continuous employment include:

- *the first 26 weeks of absence due to sickness or injury*
- *the first 26 weeks of absence due to pregnancy, and the whole of a pregnancy absence if the woman exercises her right to return*
- *the weeks between the date of an unfair dismissal and the date when the employee is reinstated or re-engaged*
- *weeks in which the employee normally worked for the employer abroad, if he returns to work in the UK.*

Although a period on strike does not count towards continuous employment, continuity is not broken by it, even where the employee was dismissed during the strike and subsequently re-engaged. Otherwise continuity is broken by any period of absence unless it is one that counts (see above). It is also normally broken by a change of employer, but not if:

- *the business of the undertaking is transferred to another employer (see TUPE, page 76)*
- *under an Act of Parliament one organisation takes over from another as the employer*
- *the employer dies and personal representatives or trustees keep on the employee in employment*
- *there is a change in the partners, personal representatives or trustees who employ the employee*
- *the employee moves to an 'associated employer' (see page 35).*

Part-timers

In addition to the major statutory rights the following rights have never been related to weekly hours and are available to all employees regardless of length of service.

These are the rights:
- to belong to a trade union and take part in its activities and the right not to belong
- to payment in insolvency
- to redundancy consultation and protective awards
- to time off with pay for antenatal care
- to maternity leave and maternity suspension
- not to be dismissed for trade union membership or activities, or for exercising statutory employment rights, or for carrying out legitimate health and safety duties.

The same is true of the right not to be discriminated against on the grounds of race or sex.

Temporary employees

Employees working on a fixed term contract for three months or less are excluded from the following rights:
- guarantee payments
- medical suspension
- minimum notice
- redundancy consultation.

Those who work for even a month are entitled to maternity suspension and to a statement of terms of employment.

PART II: COLLECTIVE RIGHTS

The Transfer of Undertakings (Protection of
  Employment) Regulations 1981
The Trade Union and Labour Relations (Consolidation)
  Act 1992
The Trade Union Reform and Employment Rights Act
  1993

TRADE UNIONS

Definitions

T1   A trade union is defined as an organisation (whether permanent or temporary) consisting wholly or mainly of workers,
whose principal purposes include the regulation of relations
between those workers and employers. The definition is,
however, worded so as to cover the union side of a joint
negotiating committee and the TUC.

T5   Only trade unions which are 'independent' benefit from most
of the rights conferred by the Acts. An 'independent trade
union' is a union 'which –

(a) is not under the domination or control of an employer or
a group of employers or of one or more employers' associations; and
(b) is not liable to interference by an employer or any such
group or association (arising out of the provision of financial or material support or by any other means whatso-
ever) tending towards such control.'

T6–9   The responsibility for deciding whether a union is independent rests with the Certification Officer (see page 138).

T119   Trade union officials are defined as including an employee
who has been elected or appointed in accordance with the
rules of the union to be a representative of the union's members in a particular company or workplace.

Comment   *The Certification Officer is given no detailed guidance by which to assess whether a union is 'under the domination or control of an employer' or 'liable to interference by an employer...' Nor is the Certification Officer concerned with whether a union is effective in representing the interests of its members, or whether it is affiliated to the TUC. The sole criterion is independence. In practice the points taken into consideration include:*

- *the union's finances, particularly its main sources of income*
- *facilities provided by the employer*
- *membership bases, particularly whether confined to a single employer*
- *union structure and the role of its officials*
- *how union policy is determined*
- *the collective bargaining record of the union.*

Most controversy has arisen over staff associations in the white-collar field. Many of these were originally established with the help of an employer but have since achieved independence and have been granted certificates.

In 1985, following the banning of existing trade unions at GCHQ (see page 97), a new staff association, the Government Communications Staff Federation, was set up, subject to the director's proviso that its constitution must be acceptable to him. In 1989 it applied for a certificate of independence to the Certification Officer who refused it. On appeal, in 1992, the EAT held that the GCSF was completely subject to the continuing approval of GCHQ's director and was 'vulnerable to interference'. The application was therefore rejected.

Since the definition of trade union officials covers workplace representatives, and since these officials are given a number of rights under the Acts, it is important that all concerned should know who they are, who they represent and what their functions are. Normal practice is for unions to notify management when shop stewards are appointed and when changes are made. Wherever possible management and unions should reach agreement on the issue of joint written credentials setting out the right and obligations of the union representatives and of management.

Ballots and elections

T 115

The Government scheme for refunding money spent by independent unions on holding secret ballots is limited to certain subjects: calling and ending strikes or other industrial actions; acceptance or rejection of an offer on pay or conditions; electing workplace representatives and any other officials or representatives called for in union rules; amending union rules; amalgamations; continuation of a political fund. The scheme, which is limited to postal ballots, is to be phased out by 1 April 1996.

Secret postal ballots are now obligatory for the following purposes:

T 51

    (a) the election of members to the union's principal executive committee,

T 77

    (b) approving the use of funds for political purposes,

TE 4

    (c) approving a union merger.

For these ballots the union must appoint an independent scrutineer, whose name must be notified to members in advance of the ballot and stated on the voting papers. He must be supplied with a copy of the relevant register of members' names and addresses which must remain confidential. The scrutineer's functions are to supervise the production and distribution of the voting papers, to act as a returning officer and to make a written report of the ballot or election.

T 230

Ballots before industrial action must also be postal and be supervised by an independent scrutineer, but are subject to more stringent requirements than those at (a) to (c) above (see page 122).

Comment   *Before 1993 an independent union could make a request to an employer to hold a secret ballot on the premises if it was on one of the subjects listed opposite, and the employer had a legal obligation to meet the request as far as was reasonably practicable. Failure to do so could lead to tribunal proceedings and payment of compensation.*

Although that obligation no longer exists, the value of workplace ballots on certain issues will remain. Employers who recognise this may wish to offer facilities to aid smooth running of the ballot: for example, by providing sealed ballot boxes; giving notice-board space for publicity; allowing reasonable time off for pre-ballot meetings. And they can ensure that those working abnormal hours, and those working away from the main establishment, have a convenient opportunity to vote.

A resolution enabling trade unions to spend money on political objects has to be renewed at least once very 10 years by a postal ballot of all members. It means that the union can set up a political fund from members' subscriptions. Members who do not wish to contribute to the political levy have to contract out. It is illegal for an employer to deduct the political levy from wages where individuals have certified in writing that they wish to contract out.

The requirements in relation to the postal ballots at (a) to (c) opposite are similar. The Act sets out the steps which a union must take in appointing an independent scrutineer and lists that person's functions. It also specifies the matters which he must cover in his report, including the number of voting papers distributed and the number returned; the number of valid votes cast for each proposition or candidate; and the number of spoiled voting papers. The scrutineer must also confirm the election arrangements to be satisfactory.

Election of union executive committees

T 46–53 With certain exceptions, the members of a union's principal executive committee (ie its governing body) must be elected by secret ballot and may not remain in office for more than five years without re-election. In this connection, and regardless of the union's rules, the president and the general secretary must be treated as members of the committee, unless they have no vote, are not union employees and hold office for no longer than three months. Also excepted are some full-time employees of the union who are nearing retirement and persons attending in a purely advisory capacity.

With the exception of certain specified groups (eg trainees and members not in employment), all members of the trade union are entitled to vote in the election, though it can be organised on a regional or trade basis. Every candidate must have the opportunity to produce his own election address (without cost to himself), and the union must send it by post with the voting paper to all those entitled to vote. The form of the addresses and their maximum length must be the same for all the candidates. The voting must be postal, secret, free from interference, convenient for the voters and without cost to them; the voting papers must be numbered; and the election must be carried out under independent scrutiny (see pages 86 and 87).

An individual member can apply to the Certification Officer or to the High Court for a declaration that the union has failed to meet these requirements. The Certification Officer must give a written reply to such an application, with reasons for the decisions. The court can make an enforcement order, demanding a postal ballot where appropriate, and if at the end of six months the union has not complied with the order, any member of the union, who was also a member when the order was made, can take further proceedings.

Comment   *Before the 1988 Act only the voting members of the principal executive had to be elected every five years. So, for example, the secretary of a union, on the committee but with no vote, could be appointed for life. This is no longer possible, but the current provisions could give rise to a different problem. These committees frequently include trained professional people, selected for their expertise – the Civil Service of the trade union movement – who need to be free to express their views rather than please the membership. Elections are unlikely to be appropriate for such appointments.*

T2–9   Trade union affairs

The affairs of trade unions are the concern of the Certification Officer who is required to keep a list of trade unions which must be made available for public inspection. To be on the list a union does not have to be independent or permanent, but it must be a union within the meaning of the Act (see page 84). Only a union which is on the list can apply for a certificate that it is independent.

T 24

T32

Unions must keep an up-to-date register of members' names and addresses and, if requested, must disclose to a member a copy of the details in it which relate to him or her. They must also keep proper accounting records and must send to the Certification Officer an annual return (see opposite). In addition, union members must receive an annual statement of income and expenditure, either personally or through a union publication. Copies of the union rules and annual returns must be available to any person on request.

Comment   *For postal ballots an up-to-date register of members and their addresses is essential. But the movement of members in and out of jobs, and in and out of unions, makes it difficult for some unions to keep accurate records.*

The information required by the Certification Officer in the unions' annual return includes revenue accounts, the current union rules, notice of any changes in the officers of the union, and details of remuneration of the president, general secretary and members of the executive.

TRADE UNION MEMBERSHIP

The right to membership

TE 14
T 174

A new heading, 'Right to membership of trade union', which had not appeared in the previous Acts, was introduced in the 1993 Act. It covers the section which provides that individuals shall not be excluded or expelled form a union except where membership is restricted to employment in a specific trade, industry or occupation, or to the possession of particular qualifications; or where the exclusion is entirely due to the individual's conduct. If an individual is not admitted to membership, application for compensation has to be made directly to the EAT. The minimum amount of compensation is such cases is £5,000.

TE 13

At the same time the Act states that inducements from an employer to make a change in his 'relationship with all or any class of his employees' (in the bargaining arrangements), shall not be regarded as 'action short of dismissal' (see below) as long as the action was such as a reasonable employer would take.

Over the years the Acts have established a number of other individual rights aimed at preventing victimisation of employees for membership or non-membership of a trade union and at protecting them from undue pressure from unions (see below).

Obligations of employers

T 146

Employees may not be subject to 'action short of dismissal' by their employers for the purpose of deterring them from membership of an independent trade union or from taking part in the activities of an independent trade union at any 'appropriate time'. Similarly, they may not be compelled by

Comment   *The effect of the changes brought about by the 1993 Act is that individuals can join the union of their choice. This right was previously limited by the law's recognition of the existence of closed shops and 'union membership agreements', under which an employee was required to belong to a specified union. A further limitation arose from the Bridlington Principles which required that unions, affiliated to the TUC, who were competing for membership in a particular area, must abide by the decision of the TUC Disputes Committee as to which union should have recruiting and negotiating rights. This was achieved by the TUC in 1939 as the most practical way to reduce multi-unionism. In 1993 there is a trend towards single-union agreements: it remains to be seen whether this will be frustrated by the new legislation, particularly when unions refuse to co-operate with each other.*

The right of an employer to offer inducements to employees to opt out of collective bargaining (in the words of the Act to make a change in his relationship with any class of his employees) had been challenged as 'action short of dismissal' (see page 95).

The provisions on 'action short of dismissal' are concerned with punitive action taken by employers against employees or potential employees. In effect they deal with the question of whether individuals who think they have been penalised for trade union membership or activities, or for non-membership, are entitled to compensation from the employer. The employee's right to be protected against such action complements the parallel pro-

their employer to join a trade union, or forced to make payments in lieu of union membership. 'Appropriate time' means any time outside the individual's working hours, or a time within working hours agreed by the employer.

T 149   An employee is entitled to complain to an industrial tribunal about infringement of these rights, and the tribunal may award compensation. It is no defence for employers to claim that they wished to avoid industrial action. But if in such a *T 150*   case industrial action, or threat of it, has been used to put pressure on an employer, the person responsible can be required by the employer or employee to be a party to the proceedings, and can be ordered to pay part or all of the compensation.

T 152   The rights of a worker in connection with trade union membership are further established by making certain kinds of dismissal unfair (see page 56). It is unfair to dismiss an employee for belonging to an independent trade union or for taking part in its activities. It is also unfair to dismiss an employee for refusing to join a union. Moreover, if employees think they have been dismissed because of union membership or activities, or because of non-membership of a union, they can take their case to an industrial tribunal regardless of their age of length of service or of the hours they work, and can also get a quick hearing (see page 60).

T 137   Discrimination in recruitment is also covered. It is unlawful to refuse to employ someone for belonging or not belonging to a trade union, and it is unlawful for an employment agency to refuse any of its services to a person on these grounds. Again, a complaint may be made to an industrial tribunal for infringement of these rights.

TE 15   An employer has no obligation to deduct union dues from *T 68*   pay, but where such a check-off arrangement exists the deduction must be authorised by the employee in writing and dated. If the amount is increased (except when due solely to an increase in wages) the employer must give one month's

Comment

visions on dismissal, and covers cases where an employee is penalised in some way other than by dismissal – for example, by denial of training opportunities, loss of promotion prospects, docking of fringe benefits, loss of overtime, withholding of pay rise, threats of dismissal – in order to force the employee to abandon union activities or to join a union. The action does not necessarily have to be taken by the employer; he would be answerable for the actions of others, such as foremen or managers, acting on his behalf.

The 1993 Act clarifies one aspect of 'action short of dismissal'. This arose from a Court of Appeal ruling that to provide incentives to those willing to sign personal contracts, and forgo union representation, amounted to unlawful action short of dismissal with the object of deterring individuals from being union members. The companies concerned had abandoned collective bargaining and were paying higher rates to employees who accepted personal contracts. Under the new provision employers can offer inducements to employees to opt out of collective bargaining and switch to individual contracts, so long as this is part of a policy to change the employee relations system, and so long as the inducements offered are reasonable. Forgoing union representation does not of course mean forgoing union membership, but if the individual is no longer part of a collective bargaining process he loses one of the main advantages of belonging to a union.

Since it is an offence to discriminate against applicants for employment on the grounds of union membership, interviewers should avoid asking questions on this subject.

The previous statutory provisions on check-off arrangements merely gave the employee the right to require the employer to stop deduction of union dues on the termination of his or her membership. The new provisions came into force on 30 August 1993. Employers already operating a check-off arrangement,

notice of the change in writing and with the reminder to the employee of his right to withdraw the authorisation at any time. Otherwise it is valid for three years.

Other provisions oblige employers to allow employees reasonable time off from work for union duties and activities (see page 46).

Obligations of unions

T 69

As explained on page 92, individuals have the right not to be excluded or expelled from a trade union. They also have the right to terminate their membership so long as they give reasonable notice and comply with any reasonable conditions.

T 65
TE 16

In addition, union members have a right not to be unreasonably disciplined by their union – that is, a right not to be disciplined for any of the following reasons:

- failing to support or take part in industrial action;
- refusing to break a contract of employment for the purposes of industrial action;
- opposing an attempt to discipline an individual unjustifiably;
- failing to agree to the deduction of union dues from pay;
- resigning from the union, or joining, or refusing to join, another;
- working with people who are not union members, or working for an employer who employs non-unionists or members of a different union;
- making an allegation in good faith that a union or a union official has acted contrary to the union's rules or has acted unlawfully;
- seeking advice from the Commissioner for the Rights of Trade Union Members, of the Certification Officer, or any other person;

Comment   *without individual written authorisation, do not have to comply until 29 August 1994.*

The recent history of GCHQ has implications for the right to belong to a trade union. In 1983, in the interests of national security, the Government banned trade unions at Government Communications Headquarters by imposing new terms and conditions of employment which permit employees to belong only to a departmental staff association approved by the Director. In addition, employees were excluded from statutory rights contained in the EP(C) Act so that they cannot claim unfair dismissal, or action short of dismissal, on grounds of trade union membership. The Civil Service Unions submitted the case to the European Commission of Human Rights whose verdict, in January 1987, was that the Government had not breached the European Convention on Human Rights. Although Article 11 guarantees the right to form associations, it also states that restrictions can be placed on freedom of association in the interest of national security 'where the rights are being exercised by members of the administration of a state.' The Commission said that the staff of GCHQ were covered by this phrase as its purpose resembled that of the police and the armed forces. This view has since been rejected by the Committee of Experts of the ILO.

The right not to be unreasonably excluded from a trade union operates independently of any other right. So individuals can make a claim against a union on the grounds that their exclusion from it contributed to their dismissal, and at the same time they can bring a claim of unfair dismissal against the employer.

97

● requesting the union to take an action required by TULC 1992.

T 64 Disciplinary action in these cases includes expulsion from the union or from any section of it; financial penalties; withholding of union benefits or facilities; encouraging another union not to accept the individual concerned as a member.

A union member who thinks he has been unjustifiably disciplined can complain within three months to an industrial tribunal and can apply for compensation.

T 63 Other provisions give a union member the right not to be denied access to the courts if his grievance has already been pursued for six months through the union's own procedures, and the right to get adequate information about the union's finances and to prevent the misuse of union property.

T 266 A Commissioner for the Rights of Trade Union Members has been appointed to assist union members in the enforcement of certain statutory rights (see page 138).

Union membership requirements in contracts

T 144

T 186

T 225

The inclusion in a commercial contract of any condition which links union membership (or non-membership) with the work to be done is prohibited. So is any attempt to use union membership or union recognition as a criterion for awarding contracts. Those who put pressure on an employer to discriminate in this way lose the immunity from legal action which is allowed in connection with trade disputes (see pages 118 and 120), as do those who organise industrial action against non-union firms – for example, by blacking non-union work.

Comment

The provisions relating to attempts to impose union membership requirements on other forms are in effect directed against trade union actions such as:

- *insisting that a 'union labour only' clause is included in a contract*
- *refusing to handle work from non-union firms*
- *refusing to work alongside non-union labour.*

As a result of the offender's loss of immunity, a person affected by such action can sue the union or its officials for damages.

COLLECTIVE BARGAINING

Recognition of trade unions

T 178   Recognition means recognition of a trade union by an employer for the purpose of collective bargaining, ie for the purpose of negotiations on one or more of the subjects included in the definition of a collective agreement (see below). Where there are disputes over recognition, ACAS can help settle them through the provision of advice and voluntary conciliation (see page 132).

An independent union which is recognised has a number of rights under the Acts – eg the right to be consulted about redundancies, the right to be given information necessary for collective bargaining, the right of officials to have paid time off for certain industrial relations duties and training, and the right to appoint the safety representatives under the Health and Safety at Work Act. Under the Transfer of Undertakings Regulations (see page 76) it also has the right to be consulted over mergers and business transfers. Also under those Regulations, any independent union recognised by the previous employer is held to be recognised to the same extent by the new one, provided the transferred undertaking keeps its distinct identity.

A commercial contract may not include a provision requiring contractors to recognise, negotiate with or consult with trade unions.

Collective agreements

T 178   A collective agreement means any agreement or arrangement made between trade unions and employers which relate to one or more of the following:

Comment *Since a number of rights depend on the union's recognition by an employer, it is essential to understand what is meant by recognition. It entails willingness to negotiate, and implies an agreement between union and employer though not necessarily a written agreement. The EAT has held that recognition need not depend on a formal relationship. It can be inferred from a course of conduct over a period of time, for example the regular discussion of wages and conditions between employer and union officials, but not from an isolated instance. And merely to apply the terms of an industry-wide agreement, without being a member of the employers' association, does not entail recognition; nor does the acceptance of a union's right to represent its members as, for example, during grievance procedures.*

The two main questions to be settled in a claim for recognition are (1) which group of workers is affected, and (2) what is the level of support for collective bargaining within that group. The first of these can be complex: for example, should all white-collar workers constitute one group or should clerical, technical and managerial employees be treated separately? In a multi-establishment company should the negotiating group be restricted to one establishment or should it be company-wide? On question (2) agreement should be reached with the union of the level of membership at which full recognition will be granted, and the extent to which facilities for union recruitment will be given in the meantime.

Before 1993, unions competing for recognition were subject to the Bridlington principles and the TUC Disputes Committee if they were affiliated to the TUC. This became irrelevant when individuals were given the right to join the union of their choice (see page 92).

The Act's definition of a collective agreement ties up with the definition of trade dispute (see page 118). As the list indicates, agreements are increasingly concerned with matters beyond the traditional 'terms and conditions' and 'procedures for avoiding disputes'. The increasing scope of collective agreements is seen in the so-called 'strike-free' agreements. It is claimed that they rep-

(a) terms and conditions of employment, or the physical conditions in which any workers are required to work;
(b) engagement or non-engagement, or termination or suspension of employment or the duties of employment, of one or more workers;
(c) allocation of work or the duties of employment as between workers or groups of workers;
(d) matters of discipline;
(e) the membership or non-membership of a trade union on the part of a worker;
(f) facilities for officials of trade unions;
(g) machinery for negotiation or consultation, and other procedures, relating to any of the foregoing matters, including the recognition by employers or employers' associations of the right of a trade union to represent workers in any such negotiation or consultation or in the carrying out of such procedures.

It can be written or oral, formal or informal.

Where a business has been transferred, the provisions of a collective agreement made by the old employer continue to apply to the individual employees covered.

T 179   Collective agreements are not in general legally binding. The assumption of the Act is that a collective agreement is not intended to be legally enforceable unless it is in writing and contains a provision to that effect. Enforceability can be limited to certain parts of an agreement if that is the wish of the parties.

T 180   The Acts clarify the position of workers who might be accused of breaking their contract of employment because they have gone on strike in breach of a procedure agreement. No-strike clauses in collective agreements, or any other clauses restricting the right of workers to take part in industrial action, cannot be treated as part of the individual's contract unless this is specifically stated in the agreement and is also incorporated (expressly or by implication) in the individ-

Comment   *resent 'a total approach to industrial relations' within a company, involving, as they do, single-union recognition, single
status, job flexibility, management commitment to consult on
key decisions, and binding 'pendulum' arbitration.*

*The broader the scope of agreements, the less amenable they will
be to legal definitions, and the less likelihood of making them
legally enforceable. Apart from any other consideration, the
actual process of enforcement, if it arose, would doubtless cause
more industrial relations problems than it solved. Nevertheless,
some of the terms of a collective agreement (eg rates of pay and
hours of work) can be made legally binding between employer
and employee if they are incorporated in the individual's contract of employment.*

*The Sex Discrimination Act 1986 makes void any discrimina-
tory provisions in collective agreements, but offers no remedy for
someone adversely affected. The 1993 Act gives the individual
the right to apply to an industrial tribunal for a declaration that
such a provision is void.*

ual contract. In addition, the agreement must be in writing and be reasonably accessible to the worker, and the unions which are party to it must be independent.

Codes of Practice

T199   ACAS has the power to issue Codes of Practice giving practical guidance for the purpose of improving industrial relations, particularly in relation to time off for trade union duties and activities, and to the disclosure of information to trade unions for the purposes of collective bargaining.

T203   The Secretary of State has a similar power to issue Codes, but with the particular purpose of promoting good practice by trade unions in the conduct of ballots and elections.

T207   A Code is not enforceable at law, but it is admissible as evidence in proceedings before an industrial tribunal or the Central Arbitration Committee.

Comment

ACAS has so far published three Codes of Practice:

1 *Disciplinary practices and procedures in employment.*
2 *Disclosure of information to trade unions for collective bargaining purposes.*
3 *Time off for trade union duties and activities (published in 1991 and superseding the 1978 version).*

Three Codes have been issued by the Employment Department:

4 *Closed Shop Agreements and Arrangements (now irrelevant because of changes to the law and revoked in 1991).*
5 *Picketing (revised in 1992).*
6 *Trade Union Ballots on Industrial Action.*

The Secretary of State's separate power to issue Codes stems from the recognition that ACAS, a tripartite body, is unable to reach agreement on certain subjects. Before issuing a Code the Secretary of State must consult ACAS.

Codes of Practice relating to other aspects of employment have also been published by:

The Manpower Services Commission (on the employment of the disabled);
The Commission for Racial Equality;
The Equal Opportunities Commission;
The Health and Safety Commission.

DISCLOSURE OF INFORMATION

General duty

T181   On request, employers have a duty to disclose to representative of independent unions they recognise information which is necessary for effective collective bargaining. Trade union representative in this connection means an official or other person who is authorised by the union to undertake collective bargaining, so could include a full-time official or a shop steward, depending on the circumstances. Guidance on disclosure is given in a Code of Practice on the subject issued by ACAS.

T182   Employers are not required to disclose information which could cause substantial injury to the company (other than by its effect on collective bargaining), nor to disclose information which is against national security or prejudicial to an individual or was received in confidence. And they will not be called upon to produce actual documents, nor to spend an unreasonable amount of time or money on preparing the information.

T183   A trade union can complain to the Central Arbitration Committee that an employer has failed to disclose information. The complaint will be referred to ACAS for conciliation, but if that fails the Committee can make a declaration as to what information is relevant and the date by which the employer must disclose it. If there is continued refusal to disclose, the

T184   union can present a claim for terms and conditions for the employees concerned and the Committee can make an award accordingly.

Comment   *The Code of Practice on disclosure of information for collective bargaining purposes gives examples of information that might be relevant in certain situations, including such items as principles and structure of payment systems; earnings and hours analysed according to work-group, grade, department, sex, etc; numbers employed; investment plans; productivity data; state of order book; gross and net profits. It emphasises that these are not intended as a checklist nor as a complete list.*

Employers and unions should try to reach agreement on the information necessary for realistic bargaining in the particular circumstances of the company, with full discussion of what is available and what could reasonably be made available. Points to consider are how, when and to whom the information should be given, and how much of it could be given on a regular basis

Information of a different kind is required by section 1 of the 1982 Employment Act (an Act which has been otherwise superceded). Aimed at improving employee involvement in companies with more than 250 employees in the UK, it states that the directors' annual report to shareholders must 'contain a statement describing the action that has been taken during the financial year to introduce, maintain and develop arrangements aimed at providing employees systematically with information on matters of concern to them as employees'.

The Safety Representatives and Safety Committees Regulations require employers to make available to safety representatives (ie union representatives) information necessary to enable them to fulfil their functions, and the Code of Practice issued under the Health and Safety at Work Act gives details of the information which should be given to them. In addition, employers with five or more employees must have a written statement of their policy on health and safety: a free leaflet giving guidance on this is available from Health and Safety Executive area offices.

Regulations made under the Social Security Act 1985 require information about occupational pension schemes to be available to members, spouses, beneficiaries and recognised trade unions. A leaflet entitled 'Disclosure of information to pension scheme members' is obtainable from the Industrial Society.

107

Information on redundancies

Employers proposing to make employees redundant must give certain information to the unions they recognise (see page 112).

Information on transfer of business

TUPE 10   Where a business is transferred from one employer to another, each has a duty under TUPE to give information about the transfer to trade union representatives, if they recognise an independent trade union in respect of any of the employees affected (see page 76).

In such cases the employer (old and new) must give the union representatives the following information:

- the approximate timing of, and reasons for, the transfer
- the legal, economic and social implications of the transfer for the employees affected
- whether any action relating to those employees is intended, including any measures which the new employer has in mind (the new employer has a duty to advise the previous employer about these).

And where action in connection with the transfer is proposed, there must be consultation with the trade union representatives of the employees affected by it. The employer must consider and answer representations made by the union representatives, and must give reasons if rejecting any.

The provisions governing failure to inform or consult in these cases are similar to those for a failure to consult about redundancies (see page 114):

(a) A trade union may complain to an industrial tribunal that an employer has failed to comply with the Regulations,

Comment

Points to note about the provision of information on the transfer of a business are:

- *it covers employees on both sides of the transaction if they are affected, not just those in the part of the business which is to be transferred*
- *it also covers employees retained in the original business if they will be affected by reorganisation following the transfer*
- *the information must be given far enough ahead to allow time for consultation on any proposed action*
- *the information must be delivered to the union representatives concerned, or sent by post.*

Points to note on the consultation aspect are:

- *the employer's duty to consult arises only if 'measures' are to be taken in respect of any of the employees affected by the transfer. (It is not clear what is meant by 'measures' but presumably any changes in work organisation, work methods, pay system and such matters would be covered.) 'Employees affected' can include individuals not being transferred*
- *since employees being transferred are no longer treated as dismissed, the need for consultation in accordance with the redundancy provisions of EPA does not arise; but it may do so in respect of employees who are not transferred but are made redundant as a result of the transfer of the business.*

and the tribunal may order the employer to pay compensation to specified groups of employees. The maximum compensation allowed is two weeks pay for each employee.

(b) An employee may complain to an industrial tribunal that the amount due under (a) above has not been paid, and the tribunal may order the employer to pay it.

PROCEDURES FOR HANDLING REDUNDANCIES

Consultation

T 188   Two duties are imposed on employers dealing with redundancies. The first is a duty to consult trade union representatives if they recognise an independent trade union in respect of the employees affected. Points to note are:

(a) the duty applies only if the trade union concerned is an independent one;

(b) consultation must take place even if only one employee is made redundant;

(c) the consultation must begin as early as possible, but where ten or more employees are affected at one establishment it must take place a minimum number of days before the first dismissals occur:

- 90 days in the case of 100 or more dismissals in a 90-day period;
- 30 days in the case of 10 or more dismissals in a 30-day period;

(d) temporary employees (ie those under a contract for three months or less) are excluded, as are those who normally work abroad.

T 188   When consulting, employers must disclose to union representatives certain information in writing, including the reasons for their proposals; the numbers and descriptions of employees affected; the proposed method of selecting the employees to be dismissed and of carrying out the dismissals; and the proposed method of calculating any non-statutory redundancy payments.

Comment   *An 'independent' trade union is defined on page 84, and the meaning of 'recognition' is discussed on page 101. A 'trade union representative' means a person authorised by the union to carry on collective bargaining with the employer in question – ie a shop steward, a district official or a national official, depending on the circumstances. The word 'establishment' is not defined: whether a particular unit can be regarded as part of a larger organisation depends on the way it is managed and the way the redundancies were decided upon.*

These redundancy rules apply regardless of length of service or of hours worked by the employees affected. An employer who has already begun consultations, and later finds it necessary to make more employees redundant, does not have to add together both lots of employees to calculate the appropriate period.

The consultation procedure does not require that the redundant employees should themselves be members of a recognised union. The determining factor is whether they are in a job or group for which a union is recognised. Non-unionists in such a job or group would be entitled to a protective award if consultation had not taken place, but they would have to rely on the union's putting in a claim on their behalf.

The EAT has held that consultation should precede the giving of notice. (This makes sense since the object of the procedure clearly is to give the unions the chance to suggest ways of avoiding the redundancy or of mitigating its effects). It has also laid down guidelines on redundancy procedures:

- *give the union as long a warning as possible*
- *consult on selection criteria, which should be capable of being objectively assessed against such matters as attendance record, efficiency at the job, experience, length of service*
- *ensure that selection is made in accordance with these criteria and consider any representations from the union about it*
- *look for alternative employment before dismissing.*

The free ACAS booklet, Redundancy Handling, *explains the key statutory requirements governing redundancy, and gives advice on the preparation and implementation of redundancy procedures.*

113

TE 34   In addition, the consultation must deal with ways of:

(i) avoiding the dismissals;
(ii) reducing the numbers to be dismissed;
(iii) mitigating the consequences of the dismissals;
and must be undertaken with a view to reaching agreement with the trade union representatives.

Notification

T 193–4   The second duty is that of notifying the Employment Department of any redundancies involving 10 or more employees at one establishment within a specific period. Points to note here are:

(a) the duty applies whether or not a union is recognised;
(b) the notice must be given a minimum number of days before the dismissals take effect – details are the same as in (c) on page 112: in both cases it is the number of dismissals at one establishment that counts;
(c) if an independent trade union is recognised in respect of the redundant employees, it must be sent a copy of the notice which must state the date when consultations with the union began;
(d) temporary employees (ie those under a contract for three months or less) are excluded, as are those who normally work abroad.

Failure to comply

These provisions are backed by a number of sanctions;

T 189   (a) A trade union may complain to an industrial tribunal that an employer has failed to consult in the way laid down, and the tribunal may make a 'protective award' which entitles every employee affected to a week's pay for each

Comment   *The information required by the Employment Department is similar to that which the employer must disclose to the unions for consultation. A leaflet on the subject and a notification form can be obtained from any local office of the Department.*

The protective award is designed to prevent instant dismissals. It represents the amount of money the employee would have received if the proper consultative procedures had been applied. If an employee unreasonably refuses an offer from the employer of a new job or a return to the old job, that individual can lose entitlement to a protective award.

An employee who accepts an offer of a different type of job is allowed a trial period (see page 70). If he leaves the new job for reasons connected with the change (eg unsuitability), the right to the protective award still applies.

In disputing a claim for a protective award, the employer has to convince the tribunal that there were special circumstances making it impracticable to consult as required, and that everything that could be done was done in the circumstances. The EAT is interpreting 'special circumstances' strictly: it has said, for example, that insolvency is not by itself a special circumstance since a company usually knows if its prospects are that bad. And the Act now states that the failure of a person controlling the employer to provide information does not constitute special circumstances: indirect control is no excuse.

Where a number of employees are involved in a protective award, it is possible for a test case to be arranged if all the parties, including the union, agree. As with unfair dismissals and other cases where a complaint has gone to an industrial tribunal, a conciliation officer must try to obtain a voluntary settlement of a redundancy issue, so making a tribunal hearing unnecessary.

week of the period specified. The period specified, ie 'the protected period', is related to the length of time which should have been allowed for consultation and cannot exceed 90 days.

T 192   (b) An employee may complain to an industrial tribunal that the amount due under a protective award has not been paid, and the tribunal may order the employer to pay it.

T 194   (c) In the case of failure to notify the Employment Department of a proposed redundancy, the Minister may institute proceedings against the employer who will be liable to a fine.

Collective agreements on redundancies

T 198   The Minister can exempt from the redundancy provisions employees who are covered by a collective agreement on redundancy, if its procedures are on the whole at least as satisfactory as those of the Act, and if it includes a right for the employee to appeal to an independent referee or to an industrial tribunal when the procedures are not followed. Application for exemption has to be made by all the parties to the agreement.

● For further information, see '*Handling redundancy*' by Sue Morris in the *Employment Law Guides* series, published by Nicholas Brealey Publishing in association with the Industrial Society.

Comment

The provision for exemption or partial exemption where there are satisfactory collective agreements is intended primarily for industries with particular problems. In the construction industry, for example, it is often very difficult to forecast completion dates and to maintain a stable labour force, and allowance may be made for this.

The employer's duties regarding redundancy payments are described on page 68.

INDUSTRIAL ACTION

T 219 The Acts do not give a right to strike. Broadly they protect from legal proceedings those involved in certain kinds of strikes – ie they give them legal immunity. Within well-defined limits, strike leaders, and organisers of other industrial action, cannot be sued for damages for the losses caused by their action. This protection arises only where a person is acting in contemplation or furtherance of a trade dispute. So the meaning of 'trade dispute' is all-important.

Trade dispute

T 244 It is defined as a dispute between workers and their employer which is wholly or mainly related to one or more of the following:

(a) terms and conditions of employment, or the physical conditions in which any workers are required to work

(b) engagement or non-engagement, or termination or suspension of employment or the duties of employment, of one or more workers

(c) allocation of work or the duties of employment as between workers or groups of workers

(d) matters of discipline

(e) the membership or non-membership of a trade union on the part of a worker

(f) facilities for officials of trade unions

(g) machinery for negotiation or consultation, and other procedures, relating to any of the foregoing matters, including the recognition by employers or employers' associations of the right of a trade union to represent workers in any such negotiation or consultation or in the carrying out of such procedures.

Comment   *Without the system of immunities, strike leaders and organisers of other forms of industrial action would be acting unlawfully, and would be in danger of being sued because they were persuading people to break contracts. The protection given to them dates from the Trade Disputes Act of 1906. In 1980 the scope of immunity was narrowed, following the widespread disruption, by blacking and picketing, of businesses only remotely connected with the source of a dispute: protection was withdrawn from certain kinds of secondary action. Later it was further narrowed by altering the definition of a trade dispute so that:*

- *it no longer covers a dispute between workers and workers, eg a dispute arising from inter-union competition for recognition in which the employer is not involved;*
- *it is now limited to a dispute between workers and their own employer, instead of between 'employers and workers', so that purely sympathetic industrial action is not covered;*
- *it has to be 'wholly or mainly related' to the matters listed opposite instead of just 'connected' with them, which is likely to affect disputes with a political element and in effect means that the courts have to be sure of the real intention behind a dispute.*

There is a trade dispute even though it relates to matters occurring outside the UK, so long as the people taking the industrial action are likely to be affected by the outcome of the dispute. And there is also one where an actual dispute is avoided by a person submitting to demands or threats.

'Worker', in relation to a dispute with an employer, does not include a former employee unless that person's termination of employment was connected with the dispute or contributed to it.

Immunities

T 219 Apart from lawful picketing, the protection against legal proceedings given to persons calling a strike, or other industrial action, is limited to action directed at the employer with whom the employees are in dispute – ie to primary action. In such a case a person acting in contemplation or furtherance of a trade dispute cannot (as a general rule) be sued for inducing another person to break a contract of any kind, or for threatening to break a contract, or for causing somebody else to do likewise. The exceptions to the general rule are listed below.

The immunity is lost by:

T 224 (a) action taken against an employer who is not a party to the trade dispute, including action by those who work under contracts for services – ie all secondary action unless it consists of lawful picketing;

T 220 (b) those who picket in an unlawful manner (see page 124);

T 222 (c) those who take industrial action to enforce trade union membership;

T 223 (d) those who take industrial action because an employee has been selectively dismissed for taking unofficial industrial action (see page 58);

Comment

A new feature in the 1980 Act's approach to immunities was the distinction that it made between primary and secondary industrial action. While recognising the trade union tradition that where primary action is not effective the next necessary step may be to stop the supply of goods to the employer in dispute, that Act withdrew immunity from such secondary action if it was used to spread disruption beyond that point – ie beyond those actively supplying goods to or receiving goods from the employer involved. The underlying principle was that secondary action is justifiable only to the extent that it is used to put direct pressure on the employer in dispute. The result was that primary action continued to have a broad immunity while secondary action, such as blacking or a sympathetic strike, had immunity only if its target was the supply of goods or services going to or from the employer in dispute during the dispute.

The 1990 Act withdrew immunity from all secondary action except secondary peaceful picketing. Thus it is still lawful to picket an employer who is not a party to the dispute (to persuade him or her, for example, not to supply or receive goods from the employer in dispute) so long as this is done in accordance with the law's definition of peaceful picketing (see page 124).

An employer in dispute does not include an associated employer (see page 35). Each employer and each dispute has to be treated separately, though cases before the courts have illustrated the difficulty of sorting out some of the organisational links between employers.

T 225   (e) those who use pressure to impose union membership or recognition requirements in commercial contracts;

T 226   (f) unions which authorise industrial action which has not been approved in a proper ballot, and those taking part in such action (see below);

T 234A
TE 21   (g) unions which have not given the proper seven days notice of the industrial action they intend to take, including information on which employees will take part (see below).

Ballots before industrial action

T 226   A union which authorises or endorses a strike or other industrial action involving breach of contract, loses its immunity at law unless, within the previous four weeks, it has held a secret ballot to test the opinion of all the members involved, and approval has been given by a majority of those voting. The ballot must either be separate for each workplace, or it can cover different places of work if all those entitled to vote are in the same occupation or grade or other bargaining group linked by common factors, and are employed by the same employer.

And to retain the immunity the following conditions must also be met:

T 226A
TE 18   (a) Unions must give employers concerned seven days notice of their intention to hold a ballot, specifying its date and the employees affected, and supplying a sample voting paper.

T 230
TE 17   (b) The ballot must be postal, secret, free from interference and without cost to the voters.

T 229   (c) The ballot paper must include the following statement – 'If you take part in a strike or other industrial action, you may be in breach of your contract of employment.' Strike action and action short of a strike must be dealt with in separate questions on the ballot paper, and these must be so framed as to require an answer 'yes' or 'no'.

Comment

Further details on ballots and elections are on pages 86–89.

Since 1988 union members have had the right to ballot on any industrial action, not just on action involving breach of the employment contract.

The four-week period mentioned opposite may be extended, up to a maximum of 12, where there are delays due to litigation and a court order is made.

In some circumstances, where those likely to be involved in industrial action have different places of work, there has to be a separate ballot for each workplace. If this occurs, the ballot must still be postal and the strict requirements on balloting must be met (see opposite).

The Employment Department Code of Practice on Trade Union Ballots on Industrial Action *sets out the legal requirements for such ballots, indicates the procedures that should normally be followed and makes recommendations about good practice. It stresses the importance of using agreed procedures, formal or informal, to avoid industrial action. In fact, many organisations might also profit from an examination of the causes of disputes, as well as an investigation into the working of existing disputes procedures, to see if they can be improved in effectiveness and speed of operation.*

T 235   (d) The ballot must include any self-employed or freelance member who might be called to take industrial action.

T 233   (e) The person or persons authorised to call the action must be specified.

T 231
TE 19   (f) Members entitled to vote must be informed of the results, as must relevant employers.

T 226B
TE 20   (g) Except where the total number entitled to vote is not more than 50, the union must appoint an independent scrutineer who must produce a report within four weeks of the ballot.

T 62   A union member can apply to the High Court for an order requiring the union to withdraw its authorisation or endorsement of industrial action if a valid ballot has not been held, and the order can specify the steps the union must take to ensure that this is done. A union can escape liability by repudiating the unlawful action in writing (see page 126), but will also have to comply with any order made by the High Court.

Picketing

T 220   Lawful picketing, 'for the purpose only of peacefully obtaining or communicating information, or peacefully persuading any person to work or abstain from working', is restricted to people attending (in contemplation or furtherance of a trade dispute) at or near their own place of work – or, if they are unemployed having lost their job in the dispute, their former place of work – and to a union official who is accompanying the members represented.

People who have no single place of work, or who normally work at a place where picketing is impracticable, are permitted to picket any premises from which they work or from which their work is administered.

Those who picket unlawfully, ie outside the above limits, lose the protection given to acts done in furthering a trade dispute and are liable to be sued for damages.

Comment

The intention of the Acts is to stop outsiders joining picket lines. In this connection, a national official of a union can accompany any members of the union who are lawfully picketing, but shop stewards can do so only if members of the particular group they represent are present.

It appears that workers (other than those who move from place to place or who work on isolated or restricted sites) have no right to picket a head office if it is situated elsewhere, and no right to picket an associated company although it may be responsible for overall policies. In the 1986 newspaper dispute, the High Court held that the pickets at the new Wapping premises were not protected by the Act since none of them had ever worked there.

There is no change in the criminal law affecting picketing. It is for the police to decide whether charges should be made for acts such as breach of the peace, obstruction of the highway and violence. Equally, picketing may still be treated as a 'nuisance' under common law if its purpose is, for example, to disrupt a business.

The Government has issued a Code of Practice on Picketing. It outlines the law on picketing and describes the role of the police in enforcing the law. It also gives guidance on the conduct of picketing.

125

Union liability

T 20   Regardless of the rule book, a union is now held responsible for any action done or authorised by:

(a) anyone empowered by the union rules to do so;
(b) the principal executive committee or the president or general secretary;
(c) any other committee of the union or any other official of the union.

T 21   The only way for the union to avoid liability for any such action is for the principal executive committee, the president or general secretary to repudiate it in accordance with the following rules. Without delay, written notice must be given to the official or committee concerned; in addition, the union must 'do its best' to give individual written notice of the repudiation to every member and employer affected. The notice to members must contain the following statement – 'Your union has repudiated any call for industrial action to which this notice relates and will give no support to such action. If you are dismissed while taking unofficial industrial action, you will have no right to complain of unfair dismissal'.

Remedies

If a union organises industrial action which is unlawful, and thereby loses its immunity, the following courses are open to those who suffer loss as a result:

Comment   *These provisions, extending a union's liability for the actions of its officials and committees are aimed at curbing 'unofficial' strikes. They make a union potentially liable for industrial action organised by any official of the union, whether employed or not and including shop stewards, and give it the choice of endorsing such action or writing to all members involved disowning it. The repudiation will not take effect if the principal executive committee, president or general secretary subsequently behave in a manner which is inconsistent with it.*

Notice of repudiation must also be given to any third party affected by the action, if requested within three months.

These provisions do not cover wildcat strikes and other industrial action organised by individuals who are not union members.

Since 1982 it has been possible to sue trade unions themselves for unlawful action, so bringing them into line with individuals such as union officials. The result is that it is possible to make a claim for damages against union funds.

(a) An employer, or anyone else whose rights have been infringed, can sue the union (or the union official responsible) at common law for an injunction to stop the action and for damages.

T 62
(b) A union member induced, or likely to be induced, to support the action can apply to the High Court for an order requiring the union to withdraw its support of the industrial action if a valid ballot has not been held; and the order can specify the steps the union must take to ensure that this is done.

T 235
TE 22
(c) Members of the public deprived, or likely to be deprived, of goods or services can apply to the High Court for an order to stop the industrial action. A new Commissioner for Protection Against Unlawful Industrial Action is available to assist potential applicants (see page 140).

A union can escape liability by repudiating the unlawful action in writing (see page 126).

Limits are set on the damages which can be awarded against a union. They range from an upper limit of £10,000 for a union with fewer than 5,000 members to £250,000 for a union with more than 100,000 members.

Where there is a trade dispute, a court order (injunction) to stop industrial action is not likely to be granted unless the person seeking it has a reasonable chance of success at the eventual trial, should it take place. And a court cannot issue an order for the suspension of the industrial action at the request of one side in a dispute (an ex-parte injunction), unless all reasonable steps have been taken to hear the views of the other side.

Comment *As long as it was only possible to sue individuals, financial redress was unlikely to be obtainable, but now claims against union funds are being made by some employers. However, an employer's primary concern is usually to get the action stopped, and an injunction (see (a) opposite) is a more effective way of doing this and avoids the delay of waiting for a trial. Failure to obey an injunction is a contempt of court, punishable by a fine and/or imprisonment.*

For the first time members of the public have the right to take proceedings in cases of unlawful industrial action, and it is immaterial whether the individual concerned has any entitlement to the goods or services affected by the industrial action. The new Commissioner will only grant assistance in certain cases, depending on such factors as whether the case is so complex that an individual could not be expected to deal with it unaided, or whether it involves a matter of substantial public interest. The assistance may include making arrangements for, or meeting the cost of, legal advice and representation.

The following points also have a bearing on industrial action:

(a) *Courts are prohibited from ordering someone to work, so an individual on strike cannot be compelled to return to work.*
(b) *A no-strike clause in a collective agreement cannot be treated as part of an individual's contract of employment unless a number of conditions are met (see page 102).*
(c) *Dismissal at the time of a strike is not unfair if all those taking part in the strike are dismissed (see page 56).*
(d) *Union members may not be disciplined by the union for defying a strike call (see page 96).*

PART III: MACHINERY

The Trade Union and Labour Relations (Consolidation) Act 1992
The Trade Union Reform and Employment Rights Act 1993

MACHINERY

The Advisory, Conciliation and Arbitration Service

The Advisory, Conciliation and Arbitration Service came into existence in 1974 and was made a statutory body in 1975. Although financed by public funds, ACAS is independent of the Government. It is controlled by a Council of nine members and a Chairman appointed by the Secretary of State. Three of the nine are appointed after consultation with the TUC, and three after consultation with the CBI.

It has a general duty to promote the improvement of industrial relations, in particular by the settlement of trade disputes through conciliation and arbitration. On request or otherwise (and at present without charge), ACAS may provide employers, employers' associations, workers and trade unions with advice on matters affecting industrial relations, and may publish general advice on such matters.

ACAS also has the power to inquire into any question relating to industrial relations in general, or in any particular industry or undertaking, and to publish its findings if publication will benefit industrial relations. And it can issue Codes of Practice containing practical guidance on industrial relations (see page 105).

If a trade dispute exists or is expected to arise, ACAS is empowered to offer conciliation and other assistance to help settle the dispute, and in doing so it is expected to make full use of existing procedural arrangements. With the consent of all the parties to a dispute, ACAS can refer the matters in dispute to the arbitration of persons appointed for that purpose, or to the Central Arbitration Committee.

Comment   *ACAS operates from a headquarters in London (at 27 Wilton Street, SW1 7AZ) and from nine offices around the country. It gives advice and assistance to employers and unions 'through surveys to diagnose the causes of deep-seated problems; planned series of visits (advisory projects) to assist in the implementation of improved methods and practices; short visits to discuss specific problems, and talks and seminars on industrial relations matters'. The service provided is at present free, but the power exists to charge fees, subject to Ministerial direction. This possibility is seen by some as a threat to the Service's independence and to its acceptability to employers, unions and individuals.*

ACAS advisory staff are able to give assistance on a range of subjects, from payment systems and manpower policies to all aspects of employment legislation. Many of its surveys and advisory projects have been concerned with industrial relations matters, such as recognition and negotiating procedures, and grievance, disciplinary and redundancy procedures. One form of assistance is through an independent audit of industrial relations which aims at providing a comprehensive picture of industrial relations within an organisation, and at identifying areas requiring attention.

Although in an industrial dispute ACAS offers three different approaches – conciliation, arbitration and mediation – conciliation (an attempt through discussion and negotiation to get the parties to reach their own agreement) is the preferred course.

Requests to ACAS for assistance can be made by employers, trade unions or individuals, separately or jointly. There are no formalities.

ACAS publications include a number of free Advisory Booklets on such subjects as job evaluation, payment systems, labour turnover, absence, workplace communications, personnel records, recruitment and selection, employment policies, employee appraisal, redundancy handling, as well as handbooks on discipline at work and on employment practises in small firms. ACAS has also published a guide to individual conciliation, explaining its purpose and the circumstances in which it is available.

133

In addition ACAS is responsible for individual conciliation. Before a complaint is heard by an industrial tribunal a conciliation officer of ACAS must try to obtain a voluntary settlement if there is a reasonable prospect of success, unless the parties concerned have reached a 'compromise agreement' (see opposite). This individual conciliation applies not only to unfair dismissal cases, but to all the sections of this and other Act which give individuals the right to a tribunal hearing (see below). A conciliation officer may also attempt to conciliate even before an application is made to an industrial tribunal.

Industrial tribunals

T 290–1
TE 36

The industrial tribunals were first established under the Industrial Training Act 1964. Their jurisdiction now covers cases arising from a number of other Acts, including the Equal Pay Act, the Sex Discrimination Acts, the Race Relations Act, and the Wages Act 1986, as well as the employment protection and trade union Acts. The tribunals also deal with complains from trade unions about the failure of an employer to consult them on an approaching redundancy, and hear appeals against Improvement and Prohibition Orders under the Health and Safety at Work Act.

TE 38

The Minister extended the jurisdiction of industrial tribunals to deal with breach-of-contract claims, which arise following claims following a dismissal.

Each tribunal consists of a chairman who is a lawyer, plus two lay members with relevant experience of industry. In certain cases the chairman can sit alone.

Complaints to tribunals normally have to be made within three months of the alleged offence. The period is six months in cases relating to selective re-engagement following a strike (to allow for the three-month period during which re-engagement of strikers may be unfair if it is discriminatory – see page 58), and for complaints of exclusion from union

Comment   *Under a 'compromise agreement' complaints arising from non-observance of certain statutory rights can be settled without going before an industrial tribunal and without involving a conciliation officer from ACAS. The rights involved are those regarding termination of employment, sex or racial discrimination and complaints under the Wages Act. Such an agreement has to be in writing and relate to a particular complaint; the employee must have had independent legal advice on its terms and effect; and an insurance policy must cover the risk of a claim by the employee for loss resulting from the advice.*

The procedure to be followed by industrial tribunals is laid down in the Industrial Tribunals (Rules of Procedure) Regulations. People involved in tribunal cases are given in advance a simple printed guide to what happens at a tribunal hearing and how to prepare for it. And when the hearing takes place the tribunal clerk is available to advise both sides about procedure. The emphasis is on informality and flexibility, though there are complaints of excessive legalism. Hearings are normally over in one day, and the decision and the reasons for it are usually given straight away. Costs are not normally awarded, but they can be if someone has brought a frivolous case to the tribunal or has acted unreasonably in some other way.

The 1989 Employment Act authorises the holding of pre-hearing reviews, and provides for regulations under which either party could be ordered to pay up to £150 if wishing to continue with the case.

135

membership (to give time for internal union procedures to be used – see page 92). It is also six months for claims for redundancy payment (see page 74).

TE 39 The 1993 Act makes it possible to avoid recourse to the tribunal system by the use of a 'compromise agreement' (see page 135). Previously any term in an agreement, which prevented an employee bringing a case before an industrial tribunal, was normally void.

- For further information, see *'Industrial Tribunals'* by Philip Perry in the *Employment Law Guides* series, published by Nicholas Brealey Publishing in association with the Industrial Society.

The Employment Appeal Tribunal

T 290–1
TE 37 This tribunal hears appeals on questions of law from the decisions of industrial tribunals, and in cases where the industrial tribunal has reached a 'perverse decision' in the light of the evidence. It has special powers in connection with unreasonable exclusion from a trade union and it hears appeals from decisions of the Certification Officer about the inclusion of organisations on the lists of trade unions and independent trade unions. It consists of judges and of lay members from both sides of industry. Cases are normally heard by a judge and either two or four appointed members so that the balance is preserved, but in certain cases the chairman can sit alone.

The Central Arbitration Committee

T 259 This body deals with complaints under the EPA disclosure procedure, and it arbitrates in any other disputes referred to it. Its members are experienced in industrial relations and are appointed by the Secretary of State after consultation with ACAS.

Tribunals no longer have to give a full statement of the reasons for their decisions in all cases. Decisions can now be issued in summary form, although the full version is still provided at the request of either party, and is automatically provided in cases involving sex or race discrimination, equal pay, and dismissal connected with trade union membership or non-membership.

Anyone wishing to get an idea of what to expect at a tribunal hearing can sit in on some other case. Members of the public can attend a tribunal hearing at any time.

The address of the Central Office of Industrial Tribunals is now, Southgate Street, Bury St. Edmonds, Suffolk IP33 2AQ.

The EAT has the power under TUER 1993 to make a restriction of proceedings order to stop a person, who has 'habitually and persistently and without any reasonable ground instituted vexatious proceedings', from pursuing industrial tribunal and EAT cases.

The Certification Officer

T 254

This officer is responsible for keeping a list of trade unions (and employers' associations) and copies of their rules, annual returns, etc. In addition the Certification Officer has to approve the rules governing ballots on the political objects of trade unions; must give a judgment on ballots for the election of union executive committees if an application is made; and is also responsible for administering the Government ballot scheme. The Certification Officer also decides which unions are independent. A trade union can apply for a certificate to this effect, and the officer has the power to withdraw a certificate if it is decided that a union is no longer independent. Although provided with staff and accommodation by ACAS, this officer is entirely independent in the exercise of these functions.

The address is 27 Wilton Street, London SW1X 7AZ.

The Commissioner for the Rights of Trade Union Members

T 110
T 266
TE Sch 8

Appointed under the 1988 Act, the Commissioner has the task of helping union members take legal action against their union to enforce certain specified statutory rights and to deal with alleged breaches of the union's rules or specified matters. The Commissioner may pay for legal advice and representation in such cases and, if requested, make arrangements to provide this help.

The address is Bank Chambers, 2a Rylands Street, Warrington, Cheshire WA1 1EN.

The Commissioner for Protection Against Unlawful Industrial Action

TE 22   This officer is able to give advice, financial help and other assistance to an individual contemplating proceedings against those whose unlawful industrial action has adversely affected his supply of goods and services.

INDEX

action short of dismissal 92–5
Advisory Conciliation and
    Arbitration Service (ACAS)
    100, 132–4
    Codes of Practice 104–5,
        106–7
    Discipline at Work
        Handbook 133
    Redundancy Handling
        booklet 113
antenatal care
    time off for 42
    payment for 43
apprentices
    redundancy payments 69
associated employer 35, 41
awards
    payable by employer 62–4

ballots 86–9, 122
    refunding money for 86
ballot paper, content of 122
blacking non-union work 98
Bridlington Agreement 93, 101

capability, dismissal for lack of
    54, 57
cash payments 31
Central Arbitration Committee
    106, 136
Certification Officer 84–5, 88,
    90–1, 138
check off
    arrangements for 32, 94–5
claims
    redundancy payments 74
    unlawful deductions 33
closed shop 93, 96
Codes of Practice 105–7
    disciplinary procedures 59,
        105
    disclosure of information
        105–7
    health and safety 49
    industrial action ballots 105
    picketing 105, 125
    time off for trade union
        duties 47, 105
collective agreements 100–3

collective bargaining 100–5
    disclosure of information for
        107
    inducements to opt out of
        93–5
commercial contracts
    collective bargaining and
        100
Commission for Racial Equality
    105
Commissioner for Trade Union
    Rights 98, 129, 138
compensation 62–4, 93
compromise agreements 60,
    66, 135
conciliation 59, 83
constructive dismissal 54–5
consultation
    redundancies 37, 114
    transfer of business 108–9
continuous employment 68, 81
contract of employment
    employers in breach of 55
    workers in breach of 102
contracting-in or out
    pension scheme 24–5
    political funds 86–7
counter notice 73

damages
    against trade unions 128
deductions from wages 30–2
    fixed 26–7
Department of Employment see
    Employment Department
discipline
    procedures 25
    trade unions by 96, 129
disclosure of information
    106–10
    ACAS Code on 106–7
    general duty 106
    on redundancies 108–9,
        112
    on transfer of business 76,
        108–10
discrimination 65
    awards for 62–3
    on union grounds 94–5, 97

in recruitment 94–5
dismissal
    company policy on 65, 67
    compensation for 62–4
    complaints to industrial
        tribunals 58
    constructive 55
    discrimination 65
    during strikes 56, 129
    fair 54
    lack of capability 57
    misconduct 54–7
    pregnancy 44
    procedure 57
    records, requirement for 67
    redundancy 69
    re-engagement 60–3
    reinstatement 60–3
    strikes 57–8, 126
    substantial reason for 54
    summary 57
    transfer of undertakings, on
        76
    unfair 56, 76
    without notice 53
    written statement of reasons
        26–8, 54

early retirement 69
elections, trade unions 88
employees
    claims for unfair dismissal
        58
    claims for redundancy pay
        74
    debts on insolvency 36
    redundancy payments for
        68
    rights on takeover or merger
        76
    temporary 50, 52, 82
    time off rights 46–51
    transfer of undertakings and
        76–9
    union rights of 96–9
    working mainly abroad 50,
        52, 54
    written information for
        22–9

141

employers
 insolvency of 36–7
 fines against 28
 rebates to 74
 obligations to union
  members 92–6
 transfer of undertakings and
  76–9
Employment Appeal Tribunal
 (EAT) 29, 57, 92, 113, 136
Employment Department
 Codes of Practice 105, 123,
  125
 notification of redundancy
  114–5
European Community
 contrasts and commonalities
  14
 Directives 15, 39, 77
 law making in 14–16
European Convention on
 Human Rights 97
exclusion from rights
 part-time employees 80
exclusion from unions 97
exemption
 dismissal procedures 64
 redundancy payments 74

fair dismissal 54, 57
fines 28
fixed deductions 26–7
fixed term contract
 employees on 55, 82
further employment
 offers for 70

grievance procedures 25
gross misconduct 57
guarantee payments 32–4
 exclusion from 34
 suspension of 35
 exemptions from 34

health and safety at work
 employers' duties 107
 representatives' right to time
  off 49
 unfair dismissal over 56
Health and Safety Commission
 49
Health and Safety Executive
 107

holidays, information on 23
immunities 120–22
 ballots before action 86–9,
  122–3
 loss of, 126–8
 picketing 124–5
independent trade unions 84,
 113
 recognition of 100–1
 rights of 46–7, 56, 76, 84,
  100–1, 106
industrial action 118–29
 authorised persons 124
 ballots before 86–9, 122
 legal immunity 120–2
 notification of 122
 picketing 120–1, 124–5
 primary and secondary 121
 trade dispute, definition of
  118
 union liability for 126–7
industrial relations 132
industrial tribunals 58, 78,
 134–6
 agreement to avoid
  proceedings 60, 135
 complaints over dismissal
  58–60, 78
 discrimination in
  recruitment 94
 explanatory leaflet 59
 pre-hearing review 59–61
 time limits 58, 134
information
 disclosure to employees 107
injunction 128
insolvency, employer's 36
 claims by employees 37, 52
inter-union disputes 93, 101
itemised pay statement 24

job description 22

lay-offs and short time 72–3
lock out
 dismissal during 56

maternity records 43
maternity rights 38–45
 antenatal care,
  payment for 43
 time off for 42–4
 dismissal on pregnancy
  grounds 44

duty to notify employer 40
leave 38–40
notice of return 39
redundancy 41
right to return to work 40
small firms, and 42
statutory maternity pay 39
suspension 45
with two years' service 40
medical suspension 48
misconduct 27, 54

National Insurance Fund 28
no-strike agreements 102, 129
normal retiring age 54–5
notice
 calculation of payment 53
 dismissal without 53
 employees not covered by
  52
 leaving before expiry 70
 periods 52–3
 return from maternity leave
  39
 right to pay during 52–3
part-time employees 34, 82
 temporary employees 82
pay statement, itemised 24–6
payment in lieu of notice 52
pension schemes 107
periods of notice 52–3
picketing 120–1, 124–5
 Code of Practice on 125
 secondary 120–1
political levy 87
postal ballots 86
pregnancy
 dismissal 44
 rights relating to 45
pre-hearing review 59–61
primary action 121
protective award 37, 114–5

Race Relations Act 1976 65
rebates to employers 74
recognition, union 100–1
redundancy
 collective 112–7
 dismissal for 69
 failure to comply 114
 leaving before end of notice
  70

making a claim 74
maternity rights 41
non-unionists 113
procedures for handling
    112–7
    consultation 112–4
    EAT guidelines 113
    notification 114–5
short-time working 35, 72
redundancy payments 68–75
    age limits for entitlements
        68
    calculating payment 68
    claiming for 74
    collective agreements 116
    exemption from 74
    further employment 70–1
    ineligibility for 68
    lay–offs and short time
        72–3
    maximum figure 68
    rebates to employers 74
    strikes during notice 72
    union consultation 37, 114
    written explanation of 28–9
re-engagement after dismissal
    60–3
reinstatement after dismissal
    60–3
retail employment
    deductions from wages 31
retiring age 55
return to work
    dismissal 60–1
    maternity 40
right to pay during notice 53

safety representatives 107
    right to time off 49
salaries, deductions from 30–2
scrutineer 86–7
secondary picketing 120–1
secret ballots 86–88
sex discrimination 65
Sex Discrimination Act 1986
    103
short time 72
    redundancy payments 72
single union agreements 93
Social Charter 17
Social Security Act 1986 41
special awards 64–5
staff associations 85

statutory maternity pay 39, 41,
    43
strikes (see also industrial action)
    dismissal during 56, 129
    during notice 72
    unofficial 127, 129
summary dismissal 57, 59
Sunday working 50
supervisors 65
suspension
    maternity 44
    medical 48

temporary employees 50, 52,
    82
terms of employment
    written particulars of 22
time off rights 46–50
    antenatal care 42
    infringement of 50
    looking for work 48–9
    public duties 46–7
    safety representatives 49
    union activities 47
trade disputes 101, 118–9
trade union membership 92–9
    discrimination against 94–5
    obligations of employers
        92–3
    obligations of unions 96–7
    right to 92, 94
trade unions 84–9
    accounts 90–1
    activities
    affairs 90–1
    annual return 90–1
    ballots and elections 86–9,
        122
    banning of at GCHQ 85, 97
    collective agreements
        100–3
    collective bargaining 100–3
    damages against 128
    definitions 84–5
    disciplinary action by 96,
        129
    exclusion from 97
    independent 84–5
    liability 126–7
    membership see trade union
        membership
    officials 47, 84–5
    political activities 87

recognition of 100–1
register of names 90–1
strike-free agreements 101
transfer of undertakings 76–9
    disclosure of information
        108–9
    dismissal and 56, 76
    employer's duty to consult
        108–9
    independent union rights 76
    rights of employees 77–9
Transfer of Undertakings
    (Protection of Employment)
    Regulations 76–7
trial period
    agreement for 70
    refusal to allow 71
TUC Disputes Committee 93

unfair dismissal 54–67
    compensation for 62–4
    complaints to tribunals
        58–60
    danger at work 56
    exceptions to 54
    health and safety over 56
    reinstatement and re-
        engagement 60–3
    transfer of business 56
    union membership over 56,
        60
'union labour only' clause 99
unlawful deductions
    claims arising from 33
unofficial strikes 127
    public right to take action
        129

victimisation 61
voluntary redundancy 69

wages
    deductions from 30–2
    definition 31
    guarantee payment 32–5
    itemised statement
    payment 30–7
    recovery of overpayment 30
    week's pay 33
Wages Act 1986 30–1
Wages Councils 36–7
week's pay 33–5
written information by
    employers 22–9

NICHOLAS BREALEY PUBLISHING

new *books* new *business*

HIRED, FIRED OR SICK & TIRED?
A Practical Guide to Your Job Rights
Lynda Macdonald

£9.99 paperback ISBN 1 85788 106 0

MANAGING THE PENSIONS REVOLUTION
A Practical Guide to Pension Schemes
Sue Ward

£16.99 paperback ISBN 1 85788 020 X

THE NEW EMPLOYMENT CONTRACT
Using Employment Contracts Effectively
Pat Leighton & Aidan ODonnell

£14.99 paperback ISBN 1 85788 021 8

ORDER FORM

Title	ISBN	Price	Qty	Cost
Postage & Packing UK or surface mail outside UK (replace with £8.00 for Airmail)				**+ £2.95**
			TOTAL	

Titles are available from all good bookshops, OR
SEND YOUR COMPLETED ORDER TO:

Nicholas Brealey Publishing Ltd   Tel: +44 (0)171 430 0224
21 Bloomsbury Way   *Fax: +44 (0)171 404 8311*
London WC1A 2TH, UK

BY CHEQUE: I enclose a cheque (payable to Nicholas Brealey Publishing) for £ . . . .
BY CREDIT CARD: I authorise you to debit my credit card account for £ . . . .
My Access/Visa/American Express/Diners Club card number is:

Expiry date: . . . . .Tel no: . . . .

Cardholder's Name: . . . . .Signature: . . . .

Position: . . . . .Organisation: . . . .

Address: . . . . .Postcode: . . . .

Pro Forma Invoices issued on request   **Bulk Order discounts** are available